SCOTUS 2018

David Klein · Morgan Marietta
Editors

SCOTUS 2018

Major Decisions and Developments of the US Supreme Court

Editors
David Klein
Department of Political Science
Eastern Michigan University
Ypsilanti, MI, USA

Morgan Marietta
Department of Political Science
University of Massachusetts Lowell
Lowell, MA, USA

ISBN 978-3-030-11254-7   ISBN 978-3-030-11255-4   (eBook)
https://doi.org/10.1007/978-3-030-11255-4

Library of Congress Control Number: 2018967211

Cover design by Oscar Spigolon

This Palgrave Macmillan imprint is published by the registered company Springer Nature Switzerland AG
The registered company address is: Gewerbestrasse 11, 6330 Cham, Switzerland

Preface

Welcome to this new annual series on the major rulings of the Supreme Court.

Each year, the Supreme Court announces new rulings with deep consequences for our lives. The decisions this year will influence how we conduct elections, who are (or are not) our neighbors, how LGBT citizens and religious businesses interact, and how millions of public employees relate to their unions. The rulings change how some of us pay taxes and whether the government has access to the data in our cell phones. But the grounds for those decisions can be obscure. The Constitution can seem distant and difficult rather than clear and compelling. Depending on how we read and understand our laws, a claim to citizen rights or to government powers can be self-evident or utterly disputed; sometimes it is obvious from one perspective, but demonstrably wrong from another. When the Justices of the Supreme Court address these disputes, many Americans want a clear, immediate discussion of the rulings and their meaning, but it is often unavailable. This series attempts to provide that discussion as soon as possible after the major decisions of the year are announced.

Each year, this volume will discuss the Court's most important decisions and developments. Often, the rulings focus on citizen rights versus government powers under the Constitution, though sometimes the Court also settles competing understandings of the text of laws (statutory interpretation), which the volumes will also explain. When a Justice departs or a new Justice arrives, we will discuss the meaning of the change for the Court's future.

For major rulings of the Court, individual chapters by noted scholars will discuss:

1. *the details of the ruling*,
2. *what it means for legal debate*, including the rights the Constitution recognizes, the principles it represents, and especially the divisions over how our laws should be read and interpreted, and
3. when possible, *the implications of the ruling for public policy or partisan politics*.

Perhaps the core purpose of the Supreme Court is to identify the existence and limits of rights, those concepts asserted by the Declaration of Independence and upheld by the Constitution, which citizens and groups hold regardless of the will of the majority. The politics of rights—free speech rights, religious rights, gay rights, gun rights, corporate rights, immigrant rights, privacy rights, and many others—are at the heart of American democracy. Many assertions of rights are recognized, while some are revolutionary. One of the core dilemmas of our system of government is when individual citizens hold a right to decide things for themselves, or when the majority is empowered to make decisions for all of us. The Supreme Court is the last resort for those who believe that their rights have been violated, as well as for those who believe that claims to rights have been expanded too far at the expense of majority rule and necessary governance.

The Supreme Court and its rulings are both principled and political. The decisions are grounded in deep (and disputed) beliefs about how the Constitution should be understood, as well as competing perceptions of the realities of contemporary society. The Court's rulings have long-term ramifications for legal doctrines as well as for the daily lives of Americans. For these reasons, the authors in this book are scholars of both the law and of American politics. They come from diverse backgrounds, with an array of academic, legal, ideological, practical, and scholarly perspectives. The rulings they explain in the following chapters speak of the long and complex history of our constitutional conflicts, but are meant to be understood and considered by ordinary citizens. In that sense, we aim to be a useful addition to the public discussion of the Constitution and the Court.

Ypsilanti, USA   David Klein
Lowell, USA   Morgan Marietta

Contents

Notes on Contributors

Brett Curry is Professor of Political Science at Georgia Southern University. His research centers on aspects of judicial politics and decision making. His scholarship has been published in a number of journals including the *Journal of Politics, Law & Society Review, Law & Social Inquiry, American Politics Research,* and *Justice System Journal.* His coauthored book, *Decision Making by the Modern Supreme Court,* was published with Cambridge University Press in 2011. A second book, *U.S. Attorneys, Political Control, and Career Ambition,* was recently published by Oxford University Press.

Stephen M. Engel is Professor and Chair of Politics at Bates College and an Affiliated Scholar of the American Bar Foundation. His research and teaching focus on American political development, constitutional law, and LGBTQ+ politics. He has written three books: *The Unfinished Revolution: Social Movement Theory and the Gay and Lesbian Movement* (Cambridge University Press, 2001), *American Politicians Confront the Court: Opposition Politics and Changing Responses to Judicial Power* (Cambridge University Press, 2011), and *Fragmented Citizens: The Changing Landscape of Gay and Lesbian Lives* (NYU Press, 2016). He is also co-editor with Stephen Skowronek and Bruce Ackerman of *The*

Progressives' Century: Political Reform, Constitutional Government, and the Modern American State (Yale University Press, 2016). His research has appeared in *Studies in American Political Development, Law & Social Inquiry,* and *Perspectives on Politics.* His current research examines how dignity has been used in legal argumentation, especially LGBT rights litigation, and what the limits of that concept might be.

Alex Keena is Assistant Professor of Political Science at Virginia Commonwealth University in Richmond, Virginia. He is co-author of *Gerrymandering in America: The House of Representatives, the Supreme Court, and the Future of Popular Sovereignty* (Cambridge University Press, 2016, with Michael Latner, Anthony McGann, and Charles Smith). His research focuses on the intersection of election law, legislative politics, and political representation.

David Klein is Professor and Department Head at Eastern Michigan University. He served as the inaugural editor of the *Journal of Law & Courts* (2011–2017) and is the author of three books: *Making Law in the United States Courts of Appeals* (Cambridge University Press, 2002), *American Courts Explained: A Detailed Introduction to the Legal Process Using Real Cases* (West Academic Publishing 2016, with Gregory Mitchell), and *The Battle for the Court: Interest Groups, Judicial Elections, and Public Policy* (University of Virginia Press, 2017, with Lawrence Baum and Matthew Streb). With Morgan Marietta, he is co-editor of the annual *SCOTUS* series at Palgrave Macmillan on the major decisions of the Supreme Court.

Michael Latner is Professor of Political Science at California Polytechnic State University in San Luis Obispo, where he is also a faculty scholar at the Institute of Advanced Technology and Public Policy. His research on electoral institutions has been published in journals such as *Election Law Journal, Electoral Studies,* and *Comparative Political Studies,* and he is the 2017–2019 Kendall Voting Rights Fellow at the Union of Concerned Scientists. His research was recently included in the edited work *Electoral Integrity in America: Securing Democracy* (Oxford University Press) and he is co-author, with Anthony McGann, Charles Anthony Smith, and Alex Keena, of *Gerrymandering in*

America: The House of Representatives, the Supreme Court, and the Future of Popular Sovereignty (Cambridge University Press).

Morgan Marietta is Associate Professor of Political Science at the University of Massachusetts Lowell, where he studies and writes about the political consequences of belief. He is the author of four books, *The Politics of Sacred Rhetoric: Absolutist Appeals and Political Influence*, *A Citizen's Guide to American Ideology: Conservatism and Liberalism in Contemporary Politics*, *A Citizen's Guide to the Constitution and the Supreme Court: Constitutional Conflict in American Politics*, and most recently *One Nation, Two Realities: Dueling Facts in American Democracy* (Oxford University Press, with David Barker at American University), discussing the causes and consequences of our polarized perceptions of facts. He and Bert Rockman from Purdue University are the co-editors of the *Citizen Guides to Politics & Public Affairs*, a series of books from Routledge dedicated to explaining the core issues and institutions of American politics. With David Klein he is co-editor of the annual *SCOTUS* series at Palgrave Macmillan on the major decisions of the Supreme Court.

Anthony J. McGann is Professor of Politics at the University of Strathclyde. He is the author of *The Radical Right in Western Europe* (University of Michigan Press, 1997), *The Logic of Democracy: Reconciling Equality, Deliberation, and Minority Protection* (University of Michigan, 2006), and *Gerrymandering in America: The House of Representatives, the Supreme Court, and the Future of Popular Sovereignty* (Cambridge University Press, 2016, with Alex Keena, Michael Latner, and Charles Smith).

Carol Nackenoff is Richter Professor of Political Science at Swarthmore College, where she teaches constitutional law and American politics. She composed the entry on the Supreme Court for Oxford Bibliographies Online. She is the author of *The Fictional Republic: Horatio Alger and American Political Discourse* (1994) and co-editor of *Statebuilding from the Margins* (with Julie Novkov, 2014) and of *Jane Addams and the Practice of Democracy* (with Marilyn Fischer and Wendy Chmielewski, 2009). Her current research examines conflicts over the extent and terms of incorporation of women, African Americans, Native Americans, workers, and immigrants into the polity between 1875 and 1925, and the role that organized women played in pressing new definitions of public work on the American state. She received her Ph.D. from the University of Chicago.

Julie Novkov is Professor of Political Science and Women's, Gender, and Sexuality Studies at the University at Albany, SUNY. She is the author of *Constituting Worker, Protecting Women* (University of Michigan Press, 2001), *Racial Union: Law, Intimacy, and the White State in Alabama, 1865–1954* (University of Michigan Press, 2008), and *The Supreme Court and the Presidency* (CQ Press, 2013). She has co-edited *Statebuilding at the Margins* (with Carol Nackenoff), *Race and American Political Development* (with Joseph Lowndes and Dorian Warren), and *Security Disarmed* (with Bárbara Sutton).

Gilbert Orbea is a senior at Swarthmore College and an honors candidate majoring in Political Science and Economics. He is President of the Student Government Organization and a member of the Editorial Board of Small Craft Warnings, a Swarthmore literary publication where he has published poetry. He interned for the Office of Economic Policy at the U.S. Treasury Department in the summer of 2018, focusing on a results-based grant program (SIPPRA) and creating a U.S. household financial stress index. He studied constitutional law with Carol Nackenoff and plans to attend law school.

Richard Pacelle Jr. is Professor and Department Head of Political Science at the University of Tennessee. He earned his undergraduate degree at the University of Connecticut and Ph.D. in Political Science at the Ohio State University. Pacelle's primary research focus is the Supreme Court. His research includes concerns with policy evolution and the role of policy entrepreneurs in the judiciary, Supreme Court agenda building and decision-making, and inter-branch relations. His publications include five books and dozens of articles and chapters in edited volumes. Most notably, he has written about the Supreme Court's agenda and the work of the Solicitor General. His work on decision making is highlighted by *Decision Making by the Modern*

Supreme Court, published by Cambridge University Press in 2011. His fifth book, *The Supreme Court in a Separation of Powers System: The Nation's Balance Wheel,* was published in 2015. He has won numerous teaching awards including the Chancellor's Award for Teaching and the Governor's Award for Teaching in 2000 at the University of Missouri-St. Louis. While at Georgia Southern University, Pacelle garnered the University Award for Excellence in Research and Scholarship and the CLASS Award for Distinction in Scholarship.

Anthony A. Peacock is Professor and Department Head in the Political Science Department at Utah State University. He is also the Director of USU's Center for the Study of American Constitutionalism. Peacock is the author or editor of numerous books, including most recently *Vindicating the Commercial Republic: The Federalist on Union, Enterprise, and War* (Lexington Books, 2018), *How to Read the Federalist Papers* (The Heritage Foundation, 2010), *Freedom and the Rule of Law* (Lexington Books, 2010), and *Deconstructing the Republic: Voting Rights, the Supreme Court, and the Founders' Republicanism Reconsidered* (The AEI Press, 2008). Peacock has also published many articles, book chapters, and book reviews on American law and politics. Additionally, he has provided media commentary on national and state politics and has lectured on American politics and law both nationally and internationally. He recently sat on the Utah Advisory Committee to the United States Commission on Civil Rights. At Utah State Peacock has taught courses on constitutional law; constitutional theory; law and policy; law, politics, and war; and political theory.

Charles Anthony Smith is Professor of Political Science and Law at the University of California-Irvine. He received his Ph.D. from the University of California-San Diego (2004) and his J.D. from the University of Florida (1987). The unifying theme of the research is how institutions and the strategic interaction of political actors relate to the contestation over rights, law, and democracy. He has published *The Rise and Fall of War Crimes Trials: From Charles I to Bush II* (Cambridge University Press); *Gerrymandering in America: The House of Representatives, The Supreme Court, and The Future of Popular Sovereignty* (Cambridge University Press), articles in *American Journal* *of Political Science, Law & Society Review, Political Research Quarterly, Justice Systems Journal, International Political Science Review,* Judicature, *Journal of Human Rights, Election Law Journal, Studies in Law, Politics & Society, Human Rights Review, Journal of International Relations & Development,* and *New Political Science* among other journals. He has published chapters in edited volumes with Cambridge University Press, Oxford University Press, Columbia University Press, and University of Pennsylvania Press, among others. He has edited a volume for Routledge and served as guest editor for special issues of the *Journal of Human Rights* and *Human Rights Review.*

1

Introduction: The 2017–2018 Term at the Supreme Court

Morgan Marietta

The Court addressed an array of contentious constitutional questions, including gay rights versus religious liberty, public sector unions and coerced speech, digital privacy, voting rights, and, of course, the Trump travel ban. Some rulings focused on constitutional principles—their existence and application—while others focused on social facts, or the prevailing circumstances the Court must recognize in order to apply constitutional principles, especially when those facts are in contention. The changes in the membership of the Court may be the most important events of this year, with the arrival of Justice Gorsuch and the departure of Justice Kennedy. The disturbing confirmation hearings of Brett Kavanaugh as Anthony Kennedy's replacement were the final chapter of an eventful year. In the chapters that follow, noted scholars on constitutional law and American politics discuss the seven major decisions of the year, followed by three concluding discussions of Justice Gorsuch' future, Justice Kennedy's legacy, and the confirmation of Justice Kavanaugh.

M. Marietta (✉)
Department of Political Science, University of Massachusetts Lowell,
Lowell, MA, USA

© The Author(s) 2019
D. Klein and M. Marietta (eds.), *SCOTUS 2018*,
https://doi.org/10.1007/978-3-030-11255-4_1

To summarize this year's major rulings in the briefest way possible, they

1. Allow for greater presidential power over U.S. borders and immigration,
2. Provide greater protection for religious belief as a basis for denying service to LGBT citizens (though the decision is narrow, leaving the extent of those protections an open question when they conflict with the dignity of other citizens),
3. Recognize the right of public sector employees to not pay fees to unions they do not wish to support,
4. Protect the privacy of cell phone location data from government search without a warrant,
5. Allow states to levy sales tax on Internet companies who do business with state residents, regardless of the geographic location of the company,
6. Allow states to purge voter rolls of infrequent voters, and
7. Allow state legislatures to gerrymander legislative districts in a way that creates partisan disparities, outside of the oversight of the Court.

This introduction begins to identify the constitutional concepts and controversies underlying those rulings, while the chapters to follow provide more detailed discussion and perspective.

Dignity

One of the most anticipated rulings of the year responds to competing claims of gay rights and religious liberty. When a same-sex couple in Colorado attempted to order a custom wedding cake, the baker refused on religious grounds. The Colorado Civil Rights Commission found him in violation of the state law banning discrimination in public accommodations. The *political* or *partisan* meaning of the controversy is clear: greater respect and public acceptance of LGBT citizens (which liberals and Democrats favor) or greater regard for public religiosity and the liberty of religious believers to dissent from participation in secular institutions (which conservatives and Republicans favor). But the *constitutional* meaning of the controversy in regard to citizen rights and government powers is more complex.

The couple asserts the right of *dignity*, which is both powerful and difficult to define. It is not found in the Constitution itself, but is found in influential precedents of the Court on abortion, gay rights, capital punishment, and religious liberty. As Stephen Engel of Bates College argues in the chapter on *Masterpiece Cakeshop*, the ruling illustrates the limits to the doctrine of dignity championed by Justice Kennedy and the growing focus of the Court on the protection of freedom of religious expression, *also as a reflection of dignity* as well as an explicit constitutional right.[1] In this dispute, the Justices must also deal with the distinction between claims of rights *against the state* and claims of rights *against fellow citizens*. The Equal Protection Clause of the Fourteenth Amendment applies to *government* action alone; the Constitution contains no explicit guarantee that *citizens* must treat each other equally or without discrimination.[2] The *state* must do so, but citizens are more free, especially when a recognized liberty to religious exercise justifies their actions.[3] Is dignity—rather than rights that are clear in the text of the Constitution—a strong foundation for disputed claims to constitutional protection?

---

[1]Kennedy's concurrence in the *Hobby Lobby* decision—upholding the liberty of employers to resist paying for forms of birth control that raise religious objections—contains this important line: "In our constitutional tradition, freedom means that all persons have the right to believe or strive to believe in a divine creator and a divine law. For those who choose this course, free exercise is essential in *preserving their own dignity* and in striving for a self-definition shaped by their religious precepts." (italics added) *Burwell v. Hobby Lobby Stores, Inc.* 573 U.S. ___ (2014), Kennedy concurrence, pages 1–2. A brief note on citations in the volume: recent decisions have not yet been printed in the *U.S. Reports* that collect all Supreme Court decisions at the Library of Congress (so the page number in the volume is still blank, as in 573 U.S.___). To identify quotes from the recent decisions, we will use page numbers from the slip opinions issued immediately by the Court, which are readily available online at the U.S. Supreme Court website (www.supremecourt.gov/opinions). Links to opinions, oral arguments, briefs by each party, and many other details are also available at SCOTUSblog.com.

[2]Amendment XIV (1868): "No state shall make or enforce any law which shall… deny to any person within its jurisdiction the equal protection of the laws."

[3]"A fundamental tenet of our Constitution is that the government is subject to constraints which private persons are not." *Krishnas v. Lee*, Kennedy concurrence, 505 U.S. at 701 (1992).

Rights in Commerce

Masterpiece Cakeshop and several of the other cases this year raise another core question: *do rights shift when citizens engage in commerce?* When a citizen clearly holds a right that would be protected while they were in their own home or even out in the public square, does that right lessen or yield to the interests of others when that same citizen engages in commerce? In other words, do commercial relations with fellow citizens shift rights?

It is important to remember that the Civil Rights Act of 1964, which outlawed racial segregation in restaurants and hotels, was upheld under the Interstate Commerce Clause of the Constitution. Congress does not have the direct power under Article I, or even under the Equal Protection Clause, to order individual citizens to treat others equally. The Court ruled that federal regulation of race relations was allowed because segregation impeded *commerce*, which Congress can regulate under the Commerce Clause. While the power of Congress and of state legislatures rises when commerce occurs, this does not mean that citizens no longer hold rights when they engage in commerce or that the need for economic regulation automatically overrides the assertion of a right.

Perhaps the best way to understand the debate is to focus on the crucial distinction between *government powers* and *individual rights*. For government to act at all, it must have that power (and the Constitution explicitly assigns and limits government powers); then that action must not violate a right of citizens (and the Constitution recognizes many specific and broad rights). Sometimes, a government power is clear, as in the power of Congress to levy taxes (assigned in Article I, Section 8), while sometimes a power is uncertain, as in President Truman's claim during the Korean War that he could nationalize the steel industry under presidential war powers as Commander in Chief of the Army and Navy (assigned in Article II, Section 2). The Court determined that executive war powers do not extend to seizing industries so far from the theater of war.[4] Under different circumstances—like wartime, or in

---

[4] *Youngstown Sheet & Tube Co. v. Sawyer*, 343 U.S. 579 (1952), known as the Steel Seizure Case.

this case, commerce—government powers may rise. However, even if government *does* possess the requisite power, a citizen still may hold a right that cannot be violated. In the case of segregation, there is no citizen right to discriminate recognized by the Constitution, so any claim against government powers is weak. But what about circumstances in which a clear right of citizens *does* exist, yet overlaps with their engagement in commerce over which government has legitimate powers?

A famous recent example is the *Hobby Lobby* case (mentioned in footnote 1). The owners of the store are practicing Christians and publicly intend to run the store grounded in religious principles (including being closed on Sundays). But given that they hire employees in an open economy, are their religious rights limited by that engagement? Justice Ginsburg argued that "one person's right to free exercise must be kept in harmony with the rights of her fellow citizens."[5] Hence, religious rights only apply to religious organizations, but not to those that engage "in the exchange of goods or services for money beyond nominal amounts."[6] Justice Kennedy disagreed, arguing that free exercise of religion includes "the right to express those beliefs and to establish one's religious (or nonreligious) self-definition in the political, civic, and economic life of our larger community."[7] In Kennedy's view, rights are not lessened by economic connections with fellow citizens. The majority of Justices agreed with Kennedy, arguing that protecting the free-exercise rights of corporations "protects the religious liberty of the humans who own and control those companies."[8]

The profit motive and other motives can either be conjoined or the one precludes the other. Can rights be asserted only if they are the primary objective, or are rights maintained when a citizen engages in

---

[5] *Hobby Lobby* Ginsburg dissent, page 28.

[6] Ibid., page 35. "The reason why is hardly obscure. Religious organizations exist to foster the interests of persons subscribing to the same religious faith. Not so of for-profit corporations. Workers who sustain the operations of those corporations commonly are not drawn from one religious community… For-profit corporations are different from religious non-profits in that they use labor to make a profit, rather than to perpetuate religious values" (pages 16, 18–19).

[7] *Hobby Lobby* Kennedy concurrence, page 2.

[8] *Hobby Lobby* decision, page 18.

commerce? If First Amendment rights to religious liberty are left out-side businesses, are free speech rights as well? What about Fourth Amendment rights against government search?

Cell phone companies can determine a phone's location with rela-tive accuracy over a long period of time. Can the company provide that information to law enforcement without the permission of the phone's owner? If a citizen signed an agreement recognizing the company's own-ership of this information, does that limit a rights claim? The problem of rights in commerce is a part of the conflict in *Carpenter v. U.S.*, this year's cell phone case on digital privacy discussed in the next chapter.

Another case that reflects the dispute over rights in commerce is *Janus*, on the power of public sector unions to charge mandatory fees. Does engaging in work for the government (in the many public sector occupations in contemporary America, from actuaries to zoologists and every job description in between) mean that First Amendment rights become limited?[9] Or do the same rights that citizens hold in other cir-cumstances still apply when working for the state?

Coerced Speech and Reliance Interests

Public sector unions have been authorized by law in several states to compel non-members to pay union fees, a practice upheld by a long-standing precedent of the Supreme Court. In *Janus v. AFSCME* (a major union representing over a million state workers), employees who object to the union's bargaining positions with the government—and especially to paying for the union's financial support of political cam-paigns—claim that mandatory union payments are a violation of Free Speech. While we normally think of the First Amendment as protecting citizens from attempts by the government to silence them, it also protects citizens from attempts by the government to *force them to speak against their will* (or in this case to fund the speech of an organization claim-ing to speak for them). In Chapter 5, Brett Curry of Georgia Southern University discusses the implications of the doctrine of coerced speech.

---

[9]For example, over half of the authors in this book are state employees.

As much as this case is about coerced speech, it is also about the *standards for overturning precedent*. *Abood v. Detroit Board of Education* has stood since 1977 as precedent for the constitutionality of mandatory service fees to unions. Justice Kagan begins the principal dissent by stating that "For over 40 years, *Abood* struck a stable balance between public employees' First Amendment rights and government entities' interests in running their workforces as they thought proper."[10] In practice, the Court can overrule its own previous decisions whenever it chooses, but in principle, the rule of *stare decisis*, or following that which has been decided, suggests that the Court should have a clear and compelling reason for change. The precedents on overruling precedent suggest that the Court should only do so when the facts on the ground have changed, or the reasoning of the prior decision was clearly wrong, or the prior ruling has become unworkable. The Court ruled in *Janus* that all of these reasons apply, and hence "*Abood* was wrongly decided and is now overruled."[11] The coerced speech inherent in mandatory payments to public sector unions "violates the First Amendment and cannot continue."[12]

One of the other major factors in the debate over the power of precedent is what are called *reliance interests*. "When the legislature, in the public sphere, and citizens, in the private realm, have acted in reliance on the previous decision," this is an additional reason to preserve the prior rule.[13] As Justice Ginsburg phrased it in her dissent in *Hobby Lobby*, Justices should be "mindful of the havoc the Court's judgment can introduce."[14] In the *Janus* case, thousands of union contracts and tremendous amounts of union revenue rely on the *Abood* precedent. Both sides agree that "the loss of payments from nonmembers may cause unions to experience unpleasant transition costs in the short term, and may require unions to make adjustments in order to attract

---

[10]*Janus v. AFSCME*, Kagan dissent, page 1.

[11]*Janus* decision, page 49.

[12]Ibid., page 48.

[13]*Janus* Kagan dissent, page 25. See also *Wayfair* decision: "Reliance interests are a legitimate consideration when the Court weighs adherence to an earlier but flawed precedent" (page 20).

[14]*Hobby Lobby* Ginsburg dissent, page 2.

and retain members," but they disagree on the constitutional meaning of this change in decades of labor practices.[15] While Justice Kagan sees the Court's decision to overrule *Abood* and uphold individual First Amendment rights as "a radically wrong understanding of how *stare decisis* operates,"[16] the majority of Justices see free speech principles as dominant over precedent and reliance interests as holding lesser importance than constitutional violations.

Digital Privacy and the Third Party Doctrine

The *Carpenter* decision on digital privacy is an example of how the Constitution and the Court deal with new situations that raise unanticipated questions of rights and powers. In Chapter 2, David Klein of Eastern Michigan University discusses the questions surrounding the use of cell phone records by law enforcement to track a citizen's location. Is the location of a cell phone something that is private and protected by the Fourth Amendment from search without a warrant, or are the electronic data that indicate a person's location owned by the phone company? In an era when citizens routinely use digital devices of several kinds to communicate and store personal information, photos, videos, emails, and even inadvertent information like their location, what aspects of these new electronic bits of data fall under the protections of the Bill of Rights and which do not?

When law enforcement suspected Timothy Carpenter of a string of robberies (ironically of Radio Shack and T-Mobile stores), his cell phone company provided the police with the location of his phone during the robberies. Grounded on that and other evidence, he and others were convicted. However, Carpenter did not give the phone company permission to reveal his records and the government did not have a warrant grounded in probable cause. Under the *third party doctrine*, the cell-phone carrier also owns and has the legal ability to give those

---

[15]*Janus* decision, page 47.
[16]*Janus* Kagan dissent, page 22.

data to the police. Because Carpenter had voluntarily used a cell phone, he no longer has control over what the company does with the data it generates. The third party doctrine comes from precedents in the 1970s dealing with bank transactions and land-line phone calls. Is it a legitimate extension of constitutional precedent to apply this concept to the new realm of cell phones and location tracking?

The majority of Justices held that "an individual maintains a legitimate expectation of privacy in the record of his physical movements."[17] The Court ruled that the electronic data contained in cell phones comprise "an intimate window into a person's life, revealing not only his particular movements, but through them his familial, political, professional, religious, and sexual associations."[18] Therefore, the third party doctrine does not apply to cell phone locations. Far beyond the specific question of data that reveal location, the emerging concerns about digital privacy extend to a broad range of questions about who owns the digital bits that we place on many forms of social media and electronic communications, from emails, to photos, to purchases. We may later delete things from public view, but they reside in electronic archives controlled by others. How we see the ownership of digital data will shape many future constitutional controversies.

Social Facts

In *Carpenter*, the Court characterized cell phones as "such a pervasive and insistent part of daily life that carrying one is indispensable to participation in modern society."[19] Hence, cell phone data are "not truly 'shared' [with the phone company] as one normally understands the term," even though users voluntarily provide a company access to revealing data by using the device.[20] If the Court had seen the prevailing

---

[17] *Carpenter* decision, page 11.
[18] Ibid., page 12.
[19] Ibid., page 17.
[20] Ibid.

facts about cell phones and electronic data differently, the ruling would likely have been quite different as well. This highlights the central role of rulings of social fact in major decisions of the Supreme Court.

In *South Dakota v. Wayfair*, the Court addresses a dispute over taxation of online purchases, which revolves around the emerging facts of the Internet. Can states charge sales tax on purchases their citizens make online, even when the retailer is located outside the state? This question has tremendous ramifications for American commerce given the boom of Internet sales. The constitutional controversy revolves *less around the extent of citizen rights* (as there is no right against taxation) and *more around the extent of government powers*: does a state have the power to tax in a way that may interfere with commerce among the states, or is regulation of *interstate* trade exclusively the province of Congress to settle at the national level? This question revolves around what is known as the Dormant Commerce Clause, reflecting a long-standing question of how much power to regulate trade is only in the hands of Congress or how much latitude an individual state can command. But Chapter 8 argues that the Court's ruling is more about its evolving understanding of *social facts*. *Wayfair* revolves around the facts of the contemporary economy in the Internet era. The Court ruled that these facts have changed, creating a company's presence in a state even when there is no *physical* presence. In this sense, "the Internet's prevalence and power have changed the dynamics of the national economy."[21] The Court corrected the "false constitutional premise" of prior decisions and broadened the powers of states to lay taxes, arguing that the social facts of the Internet—and hence of commerce—have clearly changed.[22]

Perhaps the largest challenge to the Court's ability to perceive and rule on reality comes in the gerrymandering cases of *Gill v. Whitford* and *Benisek v. Lamone*. Whether a state legislature has shifted its legislative districts in a way that intentionally benefits one party over the other is not always easy to discern. Four of the foremost scholars of these questions—Alex Keena, Michael Latner, Anthony McGann, and

---

[21] *Wayfair* decision, page 18.
[22] Ibid.

Charles Smith—explain the controversy over how the Court can know if representation is unequal enough to trigger a constitutional violation. Do we have a measurable standard or is this a political question the Court cannot decide on a reasonable basis? *Gill v. Whitford* illustrates the deep division on the Court over trust in social science expertise. During the oral arguments, Justice Sotomayor expressed a substantial degree of trust in social science: "what I'm suggesting is that this is not kind of hypothetical, airy-fairy, we guess, and then we guess again. I mean, this is pretty scientific at this point." Chief Justice Roberts, on the other hand, suggested that "you're taking these issues away from democracy and you're throwing them to the courts pursuant to, and it may be simply my educational background, but I can only describe as sociological gobbledygook."[23] Whether the Court sees the assertions of experts as gobbledygook or gold will influence many future cases that hinge on social facts.

Voting Rights

While the gerrymandering cases addressed broad concerns about voting rights when partisan vote tallies may be unconstitutionally diluted, *Husted* addresses the more direct concern of individual voters not being able to cast ballots. The Constitution leaves decisions about voting procedures to state governments, but also recognizes that individual citizens have rights to equal representation without discrimination. This tension between state control of voting regulations and individual rights to representation has arisen several times in recent constitutional controversies, especially regarding the continued constitutionality of the Voting Rights Act of 1965.[24] In Chapter 4, Richard Pacelle, Jr. of the

---

[23] *Gill v. Whitford* oral arguments transcript, 3 October 2017, pages 15, 40.

[24] *Shelby County v. Holder* (2013) invalidated the section of the Voting Rights Act that required pre-clearance by the Justice Department of changes in voting procedures in the Southern states. The Justices reasoned that the prevailing racism justifying this exercise of congressional power in 1965 was no longer the case fifty years later, another example of an empirical claim about reality the Court must evaluate.

University of Tennessee discusses the competing claims that Ohio's decision to purge voter rolls of infrequent voters was a legitimate regulation or a veiled attempt to disenfranchise minority voters, a part of what Justice Sotomayor describes in her dissent as "an unfortunate feature of our country's history."[25]

The Four Corners Doctrine and Presidential Power

The Trump travel ban raised constitutional challenges to the exclusion of immigrants and visitors from several Muslim countries such as Libya, Syria, and Yemen. The constitutional question is whether the ban is legitimately grounded in the President's broad powers as Commander in Chief under Article II and specific powers over immigration granted by Congress, or is the ban instead grounded in animus against Muslims, in violation of the First Amendment? The Court addressed what is sometimes described as the "four corners doctrine"—whether the Court should consider only the specific language and provisions of a law or executive order (within the "four corners" of the page) or whether the president's statements and actions outside this specific order should inform the Court's interpretation. In other words, is *this* president different?

The dissenters emphasize that "during his Presidential campaign, then-candidate Donald Trump pledged that, if elected, he would ban Muslims from entering the United States."[26] In their view, considering the executive order to be constitutional "leaves undisturbed a policy first advertised openly and unequivocally as a 'total and complete shutdown of Muslims entering the United States' because the policy now masquerades behind a facade of national-security concerns."[27] However, as Anthony Peacock of Utah State University explains in Chapter 7, the majority in *Trump v. Hawaii* see the travel ban as well within traditional

---

[25] *Husted* Sotomayor dissent, page 1.

[26] *Trump v. Hawaii*, Sotomayor dissent, page 4.

[27] Ibid., page 1.

presidential powers over foreign policy and border security, especially when presidential power is bolstered by federal law. According to the majority, the Immigration and Naturalization Act "exudes deference to the President in every clause."[28] The security justifications cited by the administration for restricting travel from specific countries are constitutional within the boundaries of the executive action, which should not be interpreted outside of its four corners or analyzed in light of a candidate's broader statements.[29] The Court's decision to uphold the travel ban as a reasonable security restriction will increase the power of the presidency and limit the ability of non-citizens outside the U.S. to exert constitutional protections.

Trump v. Hawaii was decided 5 to 4. So was *Janus*, as was *Husted*, all following the conservative/liberal split, with Kennedy on the conservative side with Alito, Gorsuch, Roberts, and Thomas. *Carpenter* was also decided 5 to 4, but in this case with Roberts joining the four liberal Justices (Breyer, Ginsburg, Kagan, and Sotomayor). *Wayfair* was 5 to 4 as well, but with an unusual division given its unusual focus on social facts. (Kennedy's opinion was joined by Thomas, Alito, Gorsuch, and Ginsburg, while the dissent from Roberts was joined by Breyer, Sotomayor, and Kagan.) *Masterpiece Cakeshop* went 7 to 2, pulling two liberal Justices along with the conservatives on the limited grounds of the decision.

These deeply divided decisions have established several changes in our constitutional law, raising some doctrines up and casting others down. The four corners doctrine is up, increasing presidential powers regardless of candidate statements or presidential misstatements. Rights

---

[28] *Trump v. Hawaii* decision, page 10. INA §1182(f): "Whenever the President finds that the entry of any aliens or of any class of aliens into the United States would be detrimental to the interests of the United States, he may by proclamation, and for such period as he shall deem necessary, suspend entry of all aliens or any class of aliens as immigrants" (quoted on page 10).

[29] "The Proclamation is expressly premised on legitimate purposes: preventing entry of nationals who cannot be adequately vetted and inducing other nations to improve their practices… five of the seven nations currently included in the Proclamation have Muslim-majority populations. Yet that fact alone does not support religious hostility, given that the policy covers just 8% of the word's Muslim population." Ibid., page 34.

in commerce are up, applying to religious protections but potentially broader rights as well. The power of states to regulate voting procedures is also up, regardless of concerns about discrimination or dilution of minority votes. Reliance interests are down, suggesting that the Court is willing to overturn precedent regardless of social disruption. The third party doctrine is down, allowing for greater exertions of individual control of data held by companies. And the expertise of social science is down as a means for the Court to discern evolving social facts.

These trends suggest a significant shift in the Court's guiding beliefs about the constitutional interpretation of government powers and citizen rights, especially given the changes in the membership of the Court. In Chapter 9, Carol Nackenoff and Gilbert Orbea of Swarthmore College explain the meaning of the arrival of the youngest conservative member of the Court, after this first year of Justice Neil Gorsuch's tenure on the Court. In the following chapter, Morgan Marietta of UMass Lowell discusses Justice Anthony Kennedy's unique legacy and the sea-change that his retirement signals. And in the final chapter, Julie Novkov from the University at Albany, SUNY, discusses the controversial and narrow confirmation of Justice Brett Kavanaugh and what it means for the Court. Quite a year for constitutional controversy and quite a shift in the future of the Court.

2

Carpenter v. U.S. on Digital Privacy Under the Fourth Amendment

David Klein

The ever-increasing connectivity that technology offers to us is double-edged. On the one hand, we benefit greatly from being able to reach other people or sources of information almost anytime we want. On the other hand, we sometimes wish to be truly alone, and it has become much harder for us to accomplish that. Information about where we are and even sometimes what we are doing is far more available to others than it once was.

The case of *Carpenter v. U.S.* involves the revelation of personal information to the largest and most feared "other" of all, government. When we carry around cell phones, we frequently and unknowingly transmit information about where we are to our wireless company. The essential question of *Carpenter* is how easy it should be for a government, either state or federal, to get access to that information when it suspects someone of criminal activity.

D. Klein (✉)
Department of Political Science, Eastern Michigan University,
Ypsilanti, MI, USA

© The Author(s) 2019
D. Klein and M. Marietta (eds.), *SCOTUS 2018*,
https://doi.org/10.1007/978-3-030-11255-4_2

15

The Fourth Amendment of the U.S. Constitution protects the "right of the people to be secure in their persons, houses, papers, and effects, against unreasonable searches and seizures." In many situations, to satisfy the Fourth Amendment, the government must obtain a warrant from a judge, supported by probable cause before making a search or seizure. (No one knows exactly how to define "probable cause," even the Supreme Court. Think of it as a solid reason to believe someone has committed, or is in the process of committing, a crime. It's more than just a suspicious hunch but considerably less than proof beyond a reasonable doubt.) But sometimes, a warrant isn't necessary, and sometimes the government doesn't even need probable cause. In deciding what is constitutionally required for a specific search or seizure, a court has to balance society's need to protect itself from crime against individuals' right to privacy.

Sometimes, it's an easy call. If the police suspect I might be hiding stolen gold bars in my house, they'll need to obtain a warrant to search the house by persuading a judge that there's probable cause to believe that I have the stolen bars. On the other hand, if I display the gold bars on a table at a yard sale, the police are free to come up and inspect them just like any other member of the public, no probable cause needed.

The Supreme Court's time is usually reserved for tough cases, and *Carpenter* is no exception. During an investigation of a string of store robberies in southeastern Michigan and northern Ohio, the FBI came to suspect that Timothy Carpenter had participated in the robberies. Hoping that his cell phone company's records would provide evidence that Carpenter had been near the robbery sites at the times the robberies were committed, investigators sought and received court orders directing the company to turn those records over. These court orders were not warrants supported by probable cause. They were issued under a federal statute, the Stored Communications Act, that only requires "reasonable grounds to believe that… the records or other information sought are relevant and material to an ongoing criminal investigation." Maybe the government could have persuaded a judge that there was probable cause to believe that Carpenter had participated in criminal activity, but it didn't think it had to and didn't try.

The records the government received showed the approximate location of Carpenter's phone at the beginning and end of all calls he made and received over several weeks. According to the Court, "the Government obtained 12,898 location points cataloging Carpenter's movements—an average of 101 data points per day."[1] The location information varied in its precision, placing Carpenter in "a wedge-shaped sector ranging from one-eighth to four square miles."[2]

Before his trial, Carpenter argued that the location records should be excluded because they were obtained in violation of the Fourth Amendment. He lost the argument, was convicted after a trial in which the government relied on the location evidence, and then lost the argument again in the court of appeals. But when he asked the Supreme Court to hear his case, it agreed, and this time, he won. In an opinion written by Chief Justice Roberts and joined by Justices Ginsburg, Breyer, Sotomayor, and Kagan, the Court concluded that the government's acquisition of the carrier records "invaded Carpenter's reasonable expectation of privacy in the whole of his physical movements,"[3] that it was unconstitutional for the government to obtain them without a warrant, and, therefore, that the records should not have been allowed into his trial.

Reasonable Expectation of Privacy

The phrase "reasonable expectation of privacy" is central to the majority's ruling. It comes from a 1967 case, *Katz v. U.S.*,[4] in which the Court ruled that a wiretap on a phone is a "search" in the Fourth Amendment sense of the term even though it does not involve a physical intrusion on a person's body or property. In a concurring opinion, Justice Harlan laid out a two-part test for determining when the Fourth Amendment

---

[1] *Carpenter* decision, page 3.
[2] Ibid., page 14.
[3] Ibid., page 15.
[4] 389 U.S. 347.

offers protections against an action law enforcement officials have taken or might take: (1) whether the person who is the target of the law enforcement action has "exhibited an actual (subjective) expectation of privacy"; (2) whether that expectation is "one that society is prepared to recognize as 'reasonable.'" The Supreme Court and lower courts have relied on Harlan's formulation in numerous cases since.

To illustrate how the test works, let us return to the example of the stolen gold bars. If I hide the bars in my house, I am obviously demonstrating a wish to keep them private. And almost everyone will agree that it is reasonable to expect the contents of one's own home to be private. So I meet both elements of the *Katz* test, and the Fourth Amendment will almost certainly require the police to obtain a warrant if they wish to search my house for the bars. (There are some exceptions allowing for warrantless searches under the Fourth Amendment, but they are unlikely to apply in this scenario.)

In contrast, when I set the bars out in a yard sale, I'm not demonstrating an interest in keeping them to myself. And if I said that I expected the existence of the bars to remain private, my neighbors would probably wonder if I knew what the word "private" means; they surely would not view my expectation as reasonable. Under the logic of the *Katz* test, because I have no reasonable expectation of privacy in the displayed bars, I have nothing to complain about if a police officer inspects them as any prospective buyer might. Therefore, the Fourth Amendment doesn't require the officer to get a warrant and doesn't provide me with any protection against the officer's actions. (In cases of this sort, the Supreme Court sometimes says that the contested action was not a "search" under the Fourth Amendment. That language can seem odd and confusing in some circumstances; the key thing to understand is that the police may take the action in question without obtaining a warrant or offering any special justification for proceeding without a warrant.)

The *Carpenter* case raises questions about the reasonableness of expectations of privacy in our whereabouts. None of the Justices in the majority would argue that people have a reasonable expectation of privacy in their whereabouts at every moment. For instance, when we go out in public, we know full well that we will be observed by other people. Say you are eating lunch in a restaurant. It would be silly for you to regard the fact of being in that restaurant at that time as a private matter or to claim that another diner's ordinary observation of you somehow constitutes an invasion of your privacy.

But that doesn't mean that expectations of privacy never come into play when we're in public. Let us try altering our scenario. Later in the day, you are walking in the neighborhood where you live, some distance away, and see another diner across the street, looking at you. The next morning she is there again, and in the afternoon, she is outside your workplace when you leave. The next day, you are driving somewhere and spot the same woman in a car behind you; she follows you for the rest of the trip and parks near you. Even assuming that you find nothing particularly threatening in her appearance or actions and do not fear for your safety, by this time, you are probably considering ways to make her stop, whether through confrontation or by calling the police. And surely, you won't tolerate the behavior for much longer.

The insight here is that knowing we can readily be observed at a particular moment or for a discrete span of time when in public does not make us feel okay about being watched by the same observer or observers over a long period as we move from one place to another to another. At some point, the sustained attention crosses a line into unacceptable intrusion, even if it conveys no threat. People might disagree about precisely where that line is, but almost everyone will agree that there is such a line. And while it may be difficult to say exactly why the behavior is unacceptable, no doubt most would agree that it has something to do with invasion of privacy. Applying the *Katz* test, we can conclude that while the Fourth Amendment's protections do not usually come into play when we are observed by authorities in public, they do come into play when observation becomes sufficiently pervasive.

The cell-site location information (CSLI) in *Carpenter* was less precise than in the scenario we just considered; it could only place Carpenter in a general neighborhood at any one time. But with thousands of observations, there was also a great deal more of the information. To the Justices in the majority, this much information about Carpenter, even if imprecise, was enough to cross that line into invasion of privacy. Perhaps just as importantly, they reasoned that CSLI is likely to become considerably more precise as technology develops. Because Supreme Court rulings lay out the law that lower courts are to apply in future cases and serve as guidance for the Court itself, they felt it important to protect now against that eventuality.

The Court did not announce an absolute rule requiring a warrant for every possible use of CSLI. In fact, it explicitly recognized an exception for efforts to "respond to an ongoing emergency."[5] But from now on, if authorities want to use cell location information in the course of an ordinary criminal investigation, they will normally have to get a warrant.

The Dissents

The four dissenting Justices each wrote an opinion. Two of them (Gorsuch and Thomas) were highly critical of *Katz's* expectation-of-privacy test, questioning its historical and logical foundations and arguing that judges are unable to apply it in consistent and predictable ways. In their view, the test too often boils down to whether the particular judges deciding a case personally feel that the defendant's expectations of privacy were reasonable.

Justice Thomas, who referred to the *Katz* test as a "failed experiment" that the Court "is dutybound to reconsider,"[6] argued that the right question to ask in cases like this is not whether a search occurred, but "*whose* property was searched."[7] Justice Gorsuch's proposed alternative is similar: what he referred to as "the traditional approach" of asking "if a house, paper or effect was *yours* under law."[8]

---

[5] *Carpenter* decision, page 22.

[6] *Carpenter* Thomas dissent, page 21. Many readers will be aware of Justice Thomas's reputation for seldom participating in oral arguments, but they may not be aware that he is a notably active and forceful opinion writer.

[7] Ibid., page 1.

[8] *Carpenter* Gorsuch dissent, page 12.

Despite posing similar questions, these two Justices came away with quite different views of the case. Justice Thomas was certain that Carpenter should lose, while Justice Gorsuch thought that Carpenter would have had a good chance of winning if his lawyer had addressed the right question instead of relying entirely on the *Katz* test. In an important sense, then, the division on the Court was really six Justices to three, with the six (majority plus Gorsuch) believing that it was certainly or probably wrong for the police to acquire the records here without a warrant and the others viewing the action as constitutionally unproblematic.

To understand this division properly, we need to turn our attention to two cases decided in the 1970s. In *U.S. v. Miller,* the Court ruled that bank customers have no reasonable expectation of privacy in, and therefore no Fourth Amendment protection of, their checks or other bank records.[9] In *Smith v. Maryland,* the Court reached the same conclusions about a phone company's records of the numbers dialed by a customer.[10] Central to both opinions was the understanding that the records were in the company's possession and that the contested information contained in them had been shared voluntarily with the company by the customer.

In his *Carpenter* dissent, joined by Justices Alito and Thomas, Justice Kennedy pointed out that, not only can the same be said about the location information in *Carpenter* (customers voluntarily reveal their whereabouts as a condition of connecting to and using the company's service), but CSLI is arguably considerably *less* private than the kind of information *Miller* and *Smith* open to examination. In his words, people's bank and phone call records "might disclose how much money they make; the political and religious organizations to which they donate; whether they have visited a psychiatrist, plastic surgeon, abortion clinic, or AIDS treatment center; whether they go to gay bars or straight ones; and who are their closest friends and family members."[11]

---

[9]425 U.S. 435 (1976).
[10]442 U.S. 735 (1979).
[11]*Carpenter* Kennedy dissent, pages 17–18.

Consistency and predictability in the Supreme Court's precedent are of considerable value to the people governed by it: in the area of criminal law, law enforcement officials who need to know the constitutional limits to their authority and the consequences of exceeding those limits; lawyers who have to decide what lines of argument are likely to be most effective in court; and judges who must evaluate those lines of argument to decide cases. Showing respect for its own precedent may also protect the Supreme Court's authority. For these reasons, it is reasonable to think that these three Justices were sincerely troubled by what they perceived as a break with what had been decided in the past. However, they were clearly most concerned with what the *Carpenter* decision might mean for trials and investigations in the future.

A subpoena *duces tecum* is the means by which an attorney engaged in a suit gains access to tangible evidence (including documents) possessed by a third party. Usually, the only requirements for a subpoena are that it be relevant to the case or investigation and not demand the production of so much evidence that compliance becomes overly burdensome. The effect of the *Carpenter* ruling is to impose a much more stringent requirement—a demonstration of probable cause—in some situations. The three dissenters see this as a major change in the law that will seriously undermine trial processes and, even more importantly, authorities' ability to investigate crime.

The concern about crime investigation arises because subpoenas are one of the most important tools of grand juries. The job of a grand jury is to decide if there is enough evidence against someone to justify charging them with a crime. It does not have to make that determination solely on the basis of evidence already in authorities' possession; instead, the grand jury can assist in the collection of evidence by issuing subpoenas of both people and things. The kind of evidence they can obtain from subpoenas *duces tecum* is often critical to determining whether the evidence linking someone to criminal activity is strong enough; think, for instance, of a person's purchase receipts or records of phone calls made or received.

The crucial point is that subpoenas are most valuable to a grand jury before it has probable cause to believe that a specific person committed a crime, even at times before it has probable cause to believe that a crime has been committed. It would have great trouble performing its investigative job if it had to wait for probable cause before issuing subpoenas.

The majority sought to allay these concerns, writing that the "Government will be able to use subpoenas to acquire records in the overwhelming majority of investigations. We hold only that a warrant is required in the rare case where the suspect has a legitimate privacy interest in records held by a third party."[12] However, there is no denying that the *Carpenter* decision has introduced some uncertainty into this area. Courts will face challenges in specifying exactly when and why that privacy interest exists and a warrant is required.

Looking Ahead

As it does so, the Court may need to clarify whether it really believes in the "third-party doctrine" of *Miller* and *Smith*. While only Justice Gorsuch criticized those decisions directly, the other dissenters were the only Justices to expressly defend them. The majority described its decision as declining to "extend" the doctrine to the context of cell location information. However, as the dissenters pointed out, the decision can be as easily understood as a narrowing of the doctrine's scope, in light of the similarities in facts between those precedents and the *Carpenter* case. And as one reads the majority's careful delineation of the logical underpinnings of the third party doctrine to explain why the doctrine should not apply here, it is hard to escape the feeling that they are uncomfortable with *Miller* and *Smith*.

Whatever approach the Court settles on, it will doubtless have to answer more questions about the use of CSLI. Perusing the records of a single person across an extended time is not the only way authorities might wish to use CSLI. The majority in *Carpenter* expressly declined to take a position on other possibilities, such as

---

[12]*Carpenter* decision, page 21.

tracking CSLI in real time or focusing on a certain location rather than a particular person, by downloading "information on all the devices that connected to a particular cell site during a particular interval."[13]

Most importantly, as technology becomes ever more intrusive and more precise in the information it provides about us, the Court will continue to struggle to define what intrusions go too far. The cases might be easy if we could say that technological infringements on privacy are always a bad thing or always a price we are willing to pay for safety. But we can't. Surely, most of us are willing to sacrifice at least some privacy for security cameras that discourage violent assaults or for electronic tracking that permits authorities to watch suspected terrorists and thwart their attacks. And just as surely, few of us would be willing to be observed or tracked every moment of our lives to serve those desired ends. Whether the Court continues to rely on the *Katz* test, devises something to replace it, or abandons tests altogether, it will never escape the need to determine the proper balance between society's right to protect itself by taking advantage of technological advances and an individual citizen's right to be left alone.

---

[13]Ibid., pages 17–18.

3

Gill v. Whitford on Partisan Gerrymandering

Alex Keena, Michael Latner, Anthony J. McGann
and Charles Anthony Smith

In its 2017–2018 term, the Supreme Court heard two high-profile partisan gerrymandering cases. The legality of partisan gerrymandering has been in limbo ever since *Vieth v. Jubelirer* (2004), in which the Court held that no standard currently exists for identifying unlawful partisan gerrymanders. In the aftermath of that decision, several state legislatures drew maps that were deliberately manipulated to favor one party over

A. Keena (✉)
Virginia Commonwealth University, Richmond, VA, USA

M. Latner
California Polytechnic State University, San Luis Obispo, CA, USA

A. J. McGann
University of Strathclyde, Glasgow, Scotland, UK

C. A. Smith
University of California Irvine, Irvine, CA, USA

© The Author(s) 2019
D. Klein and M. Marietta (eds.), *SCOTUS 2018*,
https://doi.org/10.1007/978-3-030-11255-4_3

another in congressional and state legislative elections.[1] So, when the Supreme Court agreed to hear two partisan gerrymandering challenges in 2017—one involving a Democratic challenge of the Wisconsin state assembly map and the other involving a Republican challenge of the Maryland congressional map—there was widespread anticipation that the Court would finally recognize a judicially discernable and manageable standard for challenging unfair partisan gerrymandering in courts. However, in both of these partisan gerrymandering cases, the Court ultimately declined to weigh in on the merits of the cases, instead sending them back to lower courts on technical grounds. The subsequent retirement of Justice Kennedy, who was widely seen as the "swing vote" on partisan gerrymandering, has led to further uncertainty about the future justiciability of partisan gerrymandering in federal courts.

Background: Redistricting Bias and the Courts

Partisan gerrymandering currently exists in a legal gray area. Although the Constitution gives the U.S. House of Representatives the power to administer its own elections, it delegates this power to the states in the absence of direction from Congress. Historically, state governments have been in charge of drawing these electoral district boundaries, a process known as "redistricting" that occurs every ten years after the census has established the size of the population. In the 1960s, the Supreme Court held that the Constitution forbids the once-common practice of "malapportionment" in redistricting, where districts have unequally sized populations. The Court held that, through the Fifth and Fourteenth Amendments, the Equal Protection Clause requires states to draw districts as equal as possible in population when they update their congressional and state legislative district maps.[2]

---

[1] See Anthony J. McGann, Charles Anthony Smith, Michael Latner, and Alex Keena, *Gerrymandering in America: The House of Representatives, the Supreme Court, and the Future of Popular Sovereignty* (New York: Cambridge University Press, 2016).

[2] *Baker v. Carr* (1962); *Reynolds v. Sims* (1964); *Wesberry v. Sanders* (1964).

These rulings fundamentally altered the politics of redistricting. Before the 1960s, states could use the drawing of malapportioned district boundaries to dilute the voting power of their political opponents. During this era, the prevalence of malapportionment in congressional maps gave an outsized influence to rural voters through the underrepresentation of urban voters. However, after 1960, state legislators could no longer dilute the voting power of their political opponents through this tactic. Unlike malapportionment, which uses population inequities to create bias, partisan gerrymandering biases electoral outcomes through the "packing" and "cracking" of voters based on their political affiliation. Here, mapmakers of one party can dilute the power of their opponents while maintaining evenly sized districts simply by concentrating their opponents into a small number of non-competitive districts ("packing") and distributing the remainder of their opponents across the remaining districts ("cracking"). The net result is that the voters of the opposition party are inefficiently distributed across the district map.

Until the 1980s, it was not clear whether extreme partisan gerrymanders could be challenged in the courts. In *Davis v. Bandemer* (1986), the Court considered but failed to resolve the question of the legality of partisan gerrymandering. The Court ruled against the Democrats who opposed an Indiana districting map but affirmed the justiciability of partisan gerrymandering. The split Court failed to articulate how such a challenge could be advanced or to establish a test that could be used to resolve partisan gerrymandering challenges.

Bandemer created many ambiguities. Although federal courts heard several partisan gerrymandering challenges in the 1990s, not a single districting plan was overturned. Nevertheless, *Bandemer* had the effect of constraining the extent of partisan gerrymandering because the threat of judicial invalidation of the maps was a real possibility. Accordingly, the districting after the 1990 and 2000 Census resulted in limited partisan bias.[3]

In *Vieth v. Jubelirer* (2004), the Supreme Court reversed its decision in *Bandemer* and threw the legality of partisan gerrymandering into jeopardy. The case addressed a Democratic challenge to the

---

[3]See McGann et al. (2016).

Pennsylvania congressional map enacted by a Republican majority in 2001. The plaintiffs claimed that the Republicans had deliberately drawn the district lines to lock the Democrats out of power. In a four-justice plurality decision, Justice Scalia asserted that the Court erred in *Bandemer* and partisan gerrymandering represented a "political question" for which the Court could not provide relief. Moreover, Scalia claimed that no standard for partisan gerrymandering that is judicially discernable and manageable exists. He argued that because the Constitution does not prohibit partisan gerrymandering, such challenges should be left to the elected branches. Justice Kennedy wrote a concurring opinion in which he agreed in part with Scalia that there currently existed no standard for detecting and adjudicating partisan gerrymandering. However, Kennedy disagreed that partisan gerrymandering is a "political question" beyond the purview of the judiciary. Instead, he suggested that one day a standard could be identified by social scientists and legal scholars.

The split decision in *Vieth* thus set the terms of future partisan gerrymandering challenges. On the one hand, because the Court cast doubt on the justiciability of partisan gerrymandering, it removed the deterrence associated with *Bandemer* that constrained the behavior of politicians in drawing extreme partisan gerrymanders. In effect, *Vieth* signaled to mapmakers that a successful partisan gerrymander challenge in the courts was highly unlikely. Legislators took note, and as a consequence, partisan bias in congressional districting spiked after the 2011 maps were enacted. On the other hand, Justice Kennedy's concurring decision left open the possibility that a suitable standard could evolve.

Partisan Gerrymandering Challenges in Wisconsin and Maryland

After the 2012 election, the full scope of partisan gerrymandering was evident when Democratic candidates for the House of Representatives took a majority of the votes, but lost control of the House to Republicans by several dozen seats. This underscored the renewed threat of partisan gerrymandering on democratic governance and federal–state relations.[4] Without intervention by the courts, state governments could effectively determine the political composition of the "People's House" and subvert the power of voters in democratic elections.

In this context, voters in several states challenged the districting plans enacted by their states as unlawful partisan gerrymanders, using a variety of novel legal theories. The common thread in all of these challenges was that they were tailored to Justice Kennedy, who was widely believed to be the "swing vote" on gerrymandering. Because Justice Kennedy staked out a middle ground in his *Vieth* opinion, legal scholars hoped to articulate a discernable and manageable legal standard for partisan gerrymandering that he would endorse.

One of the most promising was a Democratic Party challenge to the Wisconsin state assembly map that was passed by a Republican majority in the Wisconsin State Assembly. In addition to an "equal protection" challenge of the state legislative map, which argues that the harm of gerrymandering is that it undermines political equality, the novelty of this suit was that it also included a First Amendment, "free association" challenge. Moreover, the plaintiffs had consulted with expert social scientists to develop a new mathematical technique for detecting partisan gerrymanders called the "efficiency gap." The efficiency gap, they argued, represented a manageable standard for detecting unlawful partisan gerrymanders that was simple to calculate and illustrated the "harms of gerrymandering" through the use of a single number, which represents the degree to which a plan "wasted" the votes of members from one party above the other.

When a federal court ruled in favor of the plaintiffs, this represented the first time in which a federal court struck down a districting plan as an unlawful partisan gerrymander in the *Vieth* era. In legal circles and in the redistricting reform community, there was widespread anticipation that this ruling would dramatically reshape the Court's approach to the

---

[4]It is important to emphasize that partisan gerrymandering is not an inherently Republican or Democratic problem, and both parties draw partisan gerrymanders when they have the opportunity to do so. Currently, partisan gerrymandering benefits the Republican Party more so than the Democratic Party. However, this is largely because the Republicans won unified control of state government in several states in the 2010 elections.

problem. It may eventually produce a workable standard that other courts could use to evaluate similar partisan gerrymandering claims, providing a blue print for future challenges of unlawful partisan gerrymanders.

Gill v. Whitford

In 2010, for the first time in decades, Republicans won unified control of the Wisconsin General Assembly and the governorship. During the 2011 redistricting, they used their majorities to pass Act 43, a state legislative redistricting plan. The plan had the effect of diluting Democratic support, by packing Democratic voters into a minority of districts, such that after the 2012 state elections, Republicans were able to gain more than 60% of the seats in the lower house with less than 50% of the vote. A group of Democratic voters living in Wisconsin brought a suit to federal court alleging that the Republican-controlled General Assembly had wasted their votes by "packing" large majorities of Democratic voters into a small number of districts, with the intent of diluting the voting power of Democrats statewide.

In their suit, the plaintiffs asked the court to adopt the new statistical measure of an efficiency gap, which calculates statewide the difference in wasted votes between the parties as a portion of all the votes cast. The intuition behind the efficiency gap is that, if voters of one party have their votes unfairly diluted, they will have more wasted votes than the other party. Accordingly, the plaintiffs asserted that it would provide a valid method of detecting extreme partisan gerrymanders.

The plaintiffs proposed a three-prong test for detecting gerrymanders. First, the plaintiffs would need to show that the state had an intent to produce a partisan gerrymander through the district map. Second, they would also need to show that the redistrict plan resulted in an observable partisan effect, as indicated by an Efficiency Gap threshold of ±7%, which the plaintiffs claimed represents the historical boundaries of normal partisan bias in districting. Lastly, once these two conditions were met, the defense would be given the opportunity for rebuttal by showing that the partisan bias was the result of legitimate state policy or political geography. Otherwise, the plan would be considered an unconstitutional partisan gerrymander.

The plaintiffs asserted that in the case of the Wisconsin plan, partisan intent was established by the testimony of the consultant who drew the plan for the General Assembly, Political Scientist Keith Gaddie. Professor Gaddie had offered the Republican legislators a menu of options, including plans with no partisan bias. However, the majority party opted to choose a plan that gave them the largest partisan advantage. Another expert witness, Political Science Professor Kenneth Mayer, was able to draw a simulation plan that had an efficiency gap of just 2%, while the plan adopted by the General Assembly produced an estimated efficiency gap of 13%—well beyond the historical threshold proposed.

The Republican defendants responded by asserting that the efficiency gap measure amounted to a proportional representation standard, which the *Vieth* court had explicitly rejected as not being grounded in the Constitution. Moreover, they argued that the plaintiffs did not have standing to challenge the statewide plan, but rather could only challenge the individual districts in which they resided.

In its decision, the three-judge panel of the U.S. District Court for the Western District of Wisconsin noted that the *Vieth* decision meant that "the Court has not come to rest on a single, judicially manageable or discernible test for determining when the line between 'acceptable' and 'excessive' has been crossed" in terms of redistricting bias. Notwithstanding, they asserted that "the absence of a well-trodden path does not relieve us of the obligation to render a decision."[5] The court appeared to endorse the test proposed by the plaintiffs, asserting that:

> the First Amendment and the Equal Protection clause prohibit a redistricting scheme which (1) is intended to place a severe impediment on the effectiveness of the votes of individual citizens on the basis of their political affiliation, (2) has that effect, and (3) cannot be justified on other, legitimate legislative grounds.[6]

---

[5] *Whitford v. Gill*, No. 15-cv-421-bbc, 2016 WL 6837229 (W.D. Wis. 21 November 2016), page 31.
[6] Ibid., page 56.

Using this standard, the court noted Professor Gaddie's testimony suggesting "that a focal point of the drafters' efforts was a map that would solidify Republican control," and that the "the design of Act 43 ensured that the Republicans would maintain a comfortable majority."[7] Lastly, the court rejected the defense's challenge that the efficiency gap was essentially a measure of proportionality, and instead noted that, while the Constitution does not provide the right of proportional representation, it does not foreclose the possibility that proportionality can be used to indicate the existence of possible rights violations. "To say that the Constitution does not require proportional representation is not to say that highly disproportional representation may not be evidence of a discriminatory effect."[8] Moreover, the court rejected the defendants' argument that the state's political geography created conditions favorable to the Republicans. Rather, the court found the net effect of geography to be "modest" at best, rejecting the argument that this led to an "inherent advantage" that "explains Act 43's partisan effect."[9]

The lower court thus held that the Act was unconstitutional, and in a subsequent decision, ordered the General Assembly to draw a remedial map to be used in the 2018 elections. However, the defense appealed this decision to the Supreme Court, which agreed to hear the case.

Benisek v. Lamone

After the Supreme Court agreed to hear the Wisconsin gerrymandering challenge, it also agreed to hear a second case in Maryland. Although the Maryland challenge was similar in many respects to the Wisconsin case, there were two notable differences. First, the Maryland case represented a Republican challenge of a Democratic gerrymander. Second, the Maryland case involved a much more limited challenge in scope. Here, the plaintiffs challenged the legality of a single congressional

---

[7]Ibid., pages 64, 70.
[8]Ibid., page 85.
[9]Ibid., pages 91, 103.

district—the 6th district, which lies in the Western part of the state where Republican support is concentrated—rather than the map as a whole.

The original suit was filed in 2013 by a group of Republicans who charged that the state had violated their right to association under the First Amendment, as well as Article 1 of the Constitution. In 2011, Maryland had adopted a congressional redistricting plan drawn by Democratic Governor Martin O'Malley and passed by the Democratic-controlled state legislature, which gave Democrats a 7-1 seat advantage in congressional districts. Although the suit was rejected at both the district court level and in the circuit court, the Supreme Court sent the case back to the district court on appeal because the court had not properly assessed the merits of the partisan gerrymander challenge. After a second trial began in 2016, as *Shapiro v. McManus*, the panel of judges held that the plaintiffs' partisan gerrymandering claim was indeed justiciable, and the court went on to endorse a First Amendment-based standard of partisan gerrymandering. Like the lower court in *Gill*, the court asserted that the plaintiffs would have to show:

(1)   a "specific intent" by the state to impose a burden on voters based on political party,

(2)   that the state's redistricting plan has the effect of imposing an injury on the plaintiffs, in the form of vote dilution, and

(3)   a cause–effect relationship between to the two, such that the injury would not have occurred without this intent.[10]

Thus, like the Wisconsin challenge, the plaintiffs had to show that "natural" redistricting features, such as compliance with the Voting Rights Act or political geography, were not to blame, but rather intent. However, in contrast with the Wisconsin challenge, the court in the Maryland case placed the burden of proof on the plaintiffs, rather than on the state.

---

[10]*Shapiro v. McManus* (*Shapiro II*), 203 F. Supp. 3d 579 (D. Md. 2016), page 597.

Although the court embraced a partisan gerrymandering standard rooted in the First Amendment, it did not overturn the plan because the "Plaintiffs have not shown that they can likely prevail on each of the three elements of their First Amendment claim."[11] Moreover, because the Supreme Court had agreed to hear the Wisconsin case, the court decided to stay further proceedings on the case until the Supreme Court had weighed in on the matter. In response to the court's decision to suspend proceedings, the Republican plaintiffs appealed to the Supreme Court, which agreed to hear the case as *Benisek v. Lamone.*

The *Gill* and *Benisek* Decisions

Although the Supreme Court's decisions were much anticipated, they would prove disappointing to observers who had hoped that the court would use the two cases to establish a uniform standard for unlawful partisan gerrymandering. In its *Gill* decision, the Court by a 9-0 margin remanded the case back to the lower court on the grounds that the Wisconsin plaintiffs had not demonstrated standing. Because the plaintiffs in the case—Democratic voters living in Wisconsin—had failed to show that they lived in each of the individual districts being challenged, they would need to demonstrate proper standing. Thus, the Court decided not to rule on the merits of the case, but rather to send the case back to the lower court, with the possibility that the Supreme Court might hear the challenge again during a subsequent term. Shortly after releasing the *Gill* decision, the Court released the ruling in *Benisek.* Similarly, in a *per curiam* decision, the Court declined to rule on the merits of the case, remanding it back to the lower courts.[12]

Thus, the Supreme Court left the constitutionality of partisan gerrymandering open, much as it did in *Vieth.* This time around, the Court unanimously agreed that plaintiffs in the Wisconsin case did not have standing to sue, because they did not prove that they were injured in

---

[11] *Benisek v. Lamone,* 266 F. Supp. 3d 799—Dist. Court, D. Maryland 2017, page 802.

[12] A *per curiam* ("by the Court") opinion is an unsigned decision written for the Court as a whole by an unidentified Justice and without individual votes.

a "personal and individual way" within their gerrymandered districts. In this regard, the Court's decision appears to place new constraints on partisan gerrymandering challenges, which may have the effect of making it more difficult to successfully challenge a partisan gerrymander.

Writing for a unanimous court in *Gill*, Chief Justice Roberts asserts that if vote dilution, prohibited under the Fourteenth Amendment, is the alleged harm, then the plaintiffs' injury "is district specific." That is, a harm that is "personal and individual" can only injure voters within a district that has been "packed" or "cracked," such that voters outside of those districts lack standing to sue. According to Roberts, any claim that such injuries are "statewide in nature" is "a failure to distinguish injury from remedy." Moreover, claims to interests that are statewide in nature, including a voter's interest in their preferred party's strength in the legislature, are really "about group political interests, not individual legal rights."[13] This echoes what Scalia argued in *Vieth*—that parties don't have rights, only individuals do.

Roberts also explicitly rejects the statistical techniques that the plaintiffs used to demonstrate the harms of packing and cracking.

> We need not doubt the plaintiffs' math. The difficulty for standing purposes is that these calculations are an average measure. They do not address the effect that a gerrymander has on the votes of particular citizens. Partisan-asymmetry metrics such as the efficiency gap measure something else entirely: the effect that a gerrymander has on the fortunes of political parties.[14]

Thus, the plaintiffs in Wisconsin will have to show that they have been *directly* harmed (i.e., that they reside in districts that have been packed or cracked); however, they will not be able to rely upon metrics derived from statewide calculations of symmetry, such as the efficiency gap.

Justice Kagan, in her separate opinion, concurs that a claim of individual vote dilution "entails showing, as the Court holds, that [the voter] lives in a district that has been either packed or cracked." At the same

---

[13]*Gill v. Whitford* decision, page 21.
[14]Ibid., page 20.

time, she appears to accept part of the logic embodied in the original vote dilution cases, which demonstrated the individual harm to racial minority voters through malapportioned districting. She noted that in those cases, the Court "has explicitly recognized the relevance of…statewide evidence" and provided statewide remedies.[15]

As an alternative, Kagan clears a path that builds on a body of associational rights cases and First Amendment protections often favored by the Court's conservatives. She argues that party organizations should be able to defend the associational rights of their supporters. If a gerrymander "ravaged the party" that a voter supports, then the voter suffers harm, "as do all other involved members of that party."[16]

The Future of Partisan Gerrymandering Challenges

Although the Court declined to rule on the merits of partisan gerrymandering and the issue remains as thorny as it has ever been, there is a possibility that the Court will agree to address the issue again at some point in the near future. The *Gill* and *Benisek* cases are being re-litigated in lower courts, and another partisan gerrymandering challenge has succeeded in federal courts. This case, *League of Women Voters v. Rucho*, is a Democratic challenge of North Carolina's congressional map drawn by Republicans in the North Carolina General Assembly, and involves both First and 14th Amendment claims. However, it uses a different statistical technique to identify extreme gerrymanders. Like *Gill*, a federal district court ruled in favor of the plaintiffs and struck down the maps. Although the court ordered remedial maps to be implemented in advance of the 2018 U.S. House elections, that decision was stayed pending review by the Supreme Court. If the Court agrees to review

---

[15] *Gill v. Whitford* Kagan concurrence, pages 4, 7.
[16] *Gill v. Whitford* Kagan concurrence, page 9.

this case, then the plaintiffs will face a Supreme Court in which Justice Kennedy is no longer a member, with a new swing voter, presumably Chief Justice Roberts. However, Roberts has expressed skepticism with the statistical metrics developed to calculate partisan bias. Indeed, many social scientists took note when Roberts dismissed the partisan gerrymandering math as "sociological gobbledygook."[17] On the other hand, if the Court declines to hear this case, then there exists the possibility that two different federal courts will have embraced two alternative legal standards for resolving partisan gerrymandering claims.

---

[17]For example, see Michael Latner, "Sociological Gobbledygook or Scientific Standard? Why Judging Gerrymandering Is Hard," Union of Concerned Scientists Blog, 4 October 2017.

4

Husted v. A. Philip Randolph Institute on Voting Rights

Richard Pacelle

Voting rights are central to a democracy. Indeed, democracy cannot survive without them. Periodically, the news carries images of people voting in their first open, free elections. They are practically giddy. They finally have a voice. They receive an ink mark on their thumbs to show that they voted. They wear the mark like a badge of honor. They do not wash their hands. In the United States, we take the right to vote for granted. In visible presidential elections, over a third of the eligible voters do not cast a ballot. The statistics are worse in the mid-term and off-year elections: less than forty percent of the eligible voters bother to cast a ballot.

In many countries, people show up and if they have valid identification, they can vote. They do not have to register ahead of time. In the United States, that is generally not the case. Voters need to be registered before the election. Some states make it relatively easy to vote; others

R. Pacelle (✉)
Political Science Department, University of Tennessee,
Knoxville, TN, USA

© The Author(s) 2019
D. Klein and M. Marietta (eds.), *SCOTUS 2018*,
https://doi.org/10.1007/978-3-030-11255-4_4

construct obstacles. And that is why the cases before the U.S. Supreme Court like *Husted v. A. Philip Randolph Institute* (2018) are critical and have far-reaching implications.

The question in front of the Court in the case was this: when a state institutes a purge of voter registrations, when is that an allowable regulation and when does it constitute unconstitutional voter suppression? The argument in favor of the right to vote has a clear appeal: everyone should vote and it should be easy to exercise the right. But the perception is that the more restrictive the laws, the more they help the Republican Party. The easier it is to register, the better for the Democratic Party. Democrats tend to be less educated as well as younger and more mobile. In recent years, Republican state legislatures have been active in what their opponents label "voter suppression." Republicans have justified the measures as means of combatting voter fraud. Democrats claim that the incidents of fraud are wildly exaggerated and suggest that the real reason for the laws is to suppress voting among the poor, the young, and minorities.[1] Was the Ohio law in *Husted* a proper regulation or an unconstitutional violation of voting rights?

Voting Rights in America

The United States does not have a proud history of extending suffrage and voting rights. The franchise was originally limited to white male landowners. The Union had to fight (and win) a Civil War to allow African-American men to vote, but in a deal to deliver the presidency to Rutherford B. Hayes in 1876, the U.S. ended Reconstruction and left the Southern states to effectively disenfranchise black voters. And we are close to marking the 100th anniversary of women getting the right to vote in 1920.

---

[1]See Raymond Wolfinger and Steven Rosenstone, *Who Votes?* (New Haven: Yale University Press, 1980); see also Barry Burden, David Canon, Kenneth Mayer, and Donald Moynihan, "Election Laws, Mobilization, and Turnout: The Unanticipated Consequences of Election Reform," 58 *American Journal of Political Science* 95–109 (2014).

While this is not an enviable record, there have been attempts to extend the franchise. Ten of the 17 amendments to the Constitution since the Bill of Rights involve some aspect of voting.[2] Half of the ten (the 14th, 15th, 19th, 24th and 26th Amendments) were responsible for enlarging the pool of potential voters. The 15th Amendment put the constitutional stamp on the rights of minorities and authorizes Congress to pass legislation to ensure them.

Voting in some countries is compulsory and those who neglect their responsibilities can be fined. Few democracies place the responsibility of registering to vote primarily on individual citizens, rather than making the government accountable for registering eligible persons. However, the United States is one of those countries that is more restrictive. Historically, elections were seen as the province of state government, under the provisions of Articles I and II on federal elections[3] as well as the Tenth Amendment.[4] There have frequently been significant legal and practical barriers to participation. Proponents of expanded voting rights have advocated reform, but progress was slow. Reform is viewed as a zero-sum game with definite winners and losers in partisan politics and this is why it has become a major, divisive issue.

The landmark legislation to expand the franchise was the Voting Rights Act of 1965 (VRA). The VRA eliminated the most obvious obstacles to voter registration, such as literacy tests and state poll taxes.[5] The Act

---

[2]These include the 12th (election of the Vice President); 14th (recognition of citizenship allowing for voting); 15th (voting rights of minorities); 17th (direct election of Senators); 19th (voting rights of women); 20th (decreasing the time between the election and inauguration); 22nd (limit to presidential terms); 23rd (representation of Washington, DC); 24th (prohibition of poll taxes); and 26th (voting rights of young people).

[3]Article I, Section 4: "The times, places and manner of holding elections for Senators and Representatives, shall be prescribed in each state by the legislature thereof"; Article II, Section 1: "Each state shall appoint, in such manner as the Legislature thereof may direct, a number of electors...."

[4]The United States is a "federal" system with power divided between the national government in Washington and subnational governments (states and local governments). Each has its own specific powers and sometimes they share powers (like taxation, see Chapter 8). The 10th Amendment to the Constitution gives the states all powers not granted to the central government or denied to the states.

[5]The 24th Amendment ended poll taxes in federal elections, and the VRA sought to put an end to poll taxes in state elections.

imposed federal oversight of election procedures in "covered jurisdictions," like some of the former Confederate states that had historically low turnout because of racially motivated voter suppression.[6] Those states would have to "preclear" any changes to their own voting rules with the Department of Justice. The Act was immediately challenged and the Supreme Court upheld the major provisions in *Katzenbach v. South Carolina*. The impact of the VRA was impressive. In the five years after its enactment, as many African-Americans were registered to vote in the South as had been registered in the previous 100 years. In Mississippi, African-American registration increased from below 10% in 1965 to over 70% just five years later.[7]

Despite its scope, the VRA did not resolve every issue. Congress debated further corrective measures, but easing voting restrictions was presumed to have an asymmetric impact on partisan vote tallies. The conventional wisdom has been that making it easier to register and vote would help the Democratic Party much more than the Republicans.[8] The VRA would have to be periodically renewed and was in 1970, 1975, 1982, 1992, and 2006.

Ultimately, Congress passed the National Voter Registration Act (NVRA) in 1993 to make it easier for prospective voters to register. The NVRA established mail-in registration and compelled states to use existing administrative agencies to help register voters. The NVRA helped to increase voter registration, particularly for traditionally disenfranchised voters. But the implementation of the law was hardly uniform. Federal courts typically upheld the NVRA, ruling that the law was well within the power of Congress under the Fifteenth Amendment.

---

[6]The states covered in 1965 were all of Alabama, Georgia, Louisiana, Mississippi, South Carolina, Virginia, and parts of North Carolina; the Act was later extended to cover Alaska, Arizona, Texas, and parts of several other states.

[7]See Paul Joubert and Ben Crouch, "Mississippi Blacks and the Voting Rights Act of 1965," 46 *Journal of Negro Education* 157–167 (1977).

[8]For research that shows that it is hard to predict the impact of such laws, see Adam Berinsky, "The Perverse Consequences of Electoral Reform in the United States," 33 *American Politics Research* 471–491 (2005). See also Stephen Knack and James White, "Did States' Motor Voter Programs Help the Democrats?" 26 *American Politics Research* 344–365 (1988).

In the wake of the contested 2000 election, Congress pushed further reforms through the Help America Vote Act (HAVA). The new act approached voting issues from a different angle, trying to improve processes and provide resources to assist in the administration of voting in federal elections. The two acts combined were designed to remove obstacles to registration and make the act of voting easier and more reliable.

While the primary objective of the NVRA was to increase voter registration, the law had provisions for removing ineligible voters from state rolls. The legislation was aimed at leveling voting rights across the nation, but at the same time, states were designing laws that had the opposite effect: restricting voting rights. The NVRA appeared to forbid states from purging voters from registration lists simply because they did not vote in previous elections, but some states nevertheless implemented policies that did so. The stated objective for most states was to limit voter fraud. Opponents claimed that charges of fraud were exaggerated and these laws were thinly veiled attempts to disenfranchise minority and poor voters. Virtually every example of restrictive voting legislation came from Republican-controlled legislatures. Prior to recent decisions, the Supreme Court had been a bulwark for expansive voting rights. The Court supported the monitoring of Southern states that had histories of voter suppression.[9] But states continued to press and the Court began to relent.

The new waves of restrictive voting laws did not occur in a vacuum. Politically, there was a confluence of other factors and forces. Partisan polarization has become particularly acute. Republicans were very successful in winning state houses and governorships and used these as platforms to protect their ascendant status. Two strategies became popular: restrictive voting laws and gerrymandering (see Chapter 3). And the retreat of the Court dramatically altered the landscape.

In the 1980s, the Court began to retrench and even reverse some precedents. Eight years of Richard Nixon and Gerald Ford and twelve years of Ronald Reagan and George H. W. Bush bookended four

---

[9]See Richard Pacelle, *Between Law and Politics: The Solicitor General and the Structuring of Race, Gender, and Reproductive Rights Litigation* (College Station: Texas A&M University Press, 2003).

years of Democratic control under Jimmy Carter. Nixon and Reagan had four appointments each. Ford had one and Bush had two. Carter became just the fourth president to not have the opportunity to appoint at least one Justice. So Republicans had 20 years to disassemble the most liberal Court in history. Part of the reversal may also be attributed to the difficulty of the cases.[10] Because the VRA of 1965 removed overt boundaries like literacy tests and remaining state poll taxes, it was easy for the Court to strike down those types of restrictions. The second- and third-generation cases were more difficult and painted in shades of gray.

The Court reversed direction and supported restrictions on voting rights in the last decade. In *Crawford v. Marion County Election Board* (2008), the Court upheld an Indiana law that required voters to have picture identification, against claims that it was a burden on the poor and minorities. *Shelby County v. Holder* (2013) was a landmark decision that announced a significant departure. The Court struck down the pre-clearance requirements of the VRA. The Court found that preclearance was an unconstitutional burden on federalism and the sovereignty of states. The Court claimed that the preclearance of states was no longer necessary.

The *Husted* Case

This was the context when Larry Harmon was turned away from the polls. Court cases involve real people with real stories. Harmon showed up at the polls to vote in 2015 on a state ballot initiative. He had not voted in the 2012 presidential election and skipped the midterm elections before (2010) and after (2014). He was denied the opportunity to vote. He claimed that he had not received notice and wanted to remain on the rolls. With the help of the A. Philip Randolph Institute (APRI) and the American Civil Liberties Union (ACLU), Harmon challenged the purge and the law that allowed it.

---

[10]See Richard Pacelle, Brett Curry, and Bryan Marshall, *Decision Making by the Modern Supreme Court* (New York: Cambridge University Press, 2011).

The case involved the NVRA (also known as the "Motor Voter Act") of 1993 and the HAVA of 2002. Those laws were designed to make it to easier to vote and reduce the obstacles to participation. Ironically, this case involved the opposite. Embedded in the NVRA were provisions for states to remove lapsed voters from the rolls. The "Failure to Vote" Clause of the Act consists of two parts. The first part holds that states could not remove individuals from voting lists simply because they failed to vote. But the second provision says that there is nothing to stop a state from using other procedures to clear rolls. States could send post-cards to lapsed voters and after a specified time, if there was no response, the individual who had not voted could be removed from the lists.

The state of Ohio (represented by Secretary of State Jon Husted) built a "Supplemental Process" for removing voters who had not been active in the last two years. Under the NVRA, voters could not be removed solely for not voting, but the state claimed that it used the inactivity of the voters as a trigger to generate and send a confirmation notice, consistent with the federal laws. The state used a two-stage method for removing individuals who are no longer eligible to vote. First, the state employed the National Change of Address database to identify people who had moved and were no longer eligible to vote. Then state would contact the individual, who would need to return the confirmation notice to remain registered and then must vote at least once in the next four years. The "Supplemental Process" added an additional triggering device that resulted in contacting registered voters and removing them if they failed to return the notice: a failure to vote in two years.

When Larry Harmon was unable to vote because he was no longer registered, the case was taken up by the APRI. A. Philip Randolph was a civil rights activist and labor leader. The institute that bears his name is an organization for African-American trade unionists that advocates for labor, social, and economic change. The APRI was joined by the Northeast Coalition for the Homeless in challenging the provisions in the Federal District Court in Ohio. They argued that the Ohio provision violated the Motor Voter Act because it eliminated people who were not voting. They argued that the confirmation notices that were sent out were inadequate under federal laws.

The District Court held for the state of Ohio. The court ruled that using voting inactivity as a trigger did not violate the provisions of the National Motor Voter Act. The court did not address the adequacy of the confirmation notice, because Ohio agreed to change the process so it was aligned with the NVRA and HAVA.

The Randolph Institute appealed the decision to the Sixth Circuit Court of Appeals, which reversed the District Court's decision. The Court of Appeals ruled that the Ohio process amounted to the very thing the laws were trying to prevent: removing voters from eligibility because they had not voted.

The Court of Appeals vote was 2-1. Most Court of Appeals decisions come from three-judge panels and are unanimous. When the judges split 2-1, it sends a clear signal of division to the Supreme Court, enhancing the chances that case will be accepted for review. Most often, the Supreme Court accepts cases to reverse the lower court. This time, the state of Ohio appealed the judgment, and the Supreme Court agreed to hear the case.

The Friends of the Court

Any judicial decision from the lowest trial court to the Supreme Court itself has great meaning for the parties to the case. But often, decisions will have implications for a wide range of other actors. Clearly, the *Husted* case would have such a footprint. Every state, as well as millions of potential and actual voters, would be affected by the decision. This would be particularly true for those who sit out an election or two but later want to cast their vote. It is important for the Supreme Court to anticipate the implications of its decisions. One of the best ways for the Court to gauge the potential effects of a decision is through the use of the *amicus curiae* brief.

The *amicus curiae* (friend of the court) brief is presented by groups that will be affected by the decision but are not parties to the specific case before the Supreme Court. The *amicus* briefs provide the Supreme Court with an informal tally of public opinion. The state of Georgia filed an *amicus curiae* brief that was joined by 14 other states in support of Ohio. A group of former directors of the Civil Rights Division from the Department of Justice filed a brief and surprisingly also supported Ohio. On the other side, the Brennan Center (named for former Justice William Brennan, a liberal lion) filed a brief that the League of Women Voters joined. A dozen states (eleven solid blue states and Kentucky) also filed a joint *amicus* brief, arguing that the Ohio law was an unnecessary violation of voting rights and offered less drastic alternatives. They were joined by a number of other groups including Asian Americans Advocating Justice, the National Disability Rights Network, the Vote Veterans Action Foundation, and the Libertarian National Committee.

The most important voice (besides the Justices) belongs to the Solicitor General (SG) of the United States. The SG is responsible for government litigation heading to the Supreme Court. The SG decides which cases that the government lost should be appealed to the Court. The Office of the Solicitor General (OSG) also argues the cases before the Court. The OSG has unmatched success in getting cases accepted by the Supreme Court and winning on the merits.[11] The government is involved in dozens of cases each term, but even when the United States is not a party, it can enter as an *amicus curiae*. As the most successful litigant, the word of the SG carries tremendous weight. In the *Husted* case, the SG (under President Obama) entered the case originally on behalf of the Randolph Institute and against the state. But with the election of Donald Trump, the OSG took the rare step of changing positions in the case to support Ohio.

There was good reason to think that the supplementary procedures used by the state of Ohio would survive Supreme Court review. Recent Supreme Court precedents had given states considerable and increasing leeway in writing their own election laws and had removed the preclearance requirements. In addition, the Supreme Court leaned to the right: conservative Justices outnumbered their liberal colleagues.

---

[11]See Pacelle, *Between Law & Politics*.

The Decision

A number of states had similar laws, but the Ohio version was considered the most aggressive in purging voters. The *amicus curiae* brief filed by the Brennan Center argued that only Ohio "commences such a process based on the failure to vote in a single federal election cycle," adding that "literally every other state uses a different, and more voter-protective, practice."

The challenge to the Ohio Supplemental Procedure was based on the language of Federal laws that expressly prohibit states from removing people from the rolls simply because they failed to vote. But the Court ruled 5-4 that the laws *did* allow election officials who suspect a voter has moved to send a confirmation notice. And the failure to return the notice or vote in subsequent elections made the non-voter subject to a purge.

In the majority opinion of the Court, Justice Samuel Alito pointed to research that supported congressional and state efforts to clean up voting rolls. Alito quoted a study that showed that an estimated 24 million voter registrations were inaccurate or invalid and that close to three million people were registered to vote in more than one state.

Federal law, Justice Alito wrote, "plainly reflects Congress's judgment that the failure to send back the card, coupled with the failure to vote during the period covering the next two general federal elections, is significant evidence that the addressee has moved."[12] Justice Alito urged deference to Congress and accused the dissenters of having a policy disagreement with the legislatures. He wrote that the case "presents a question of statutory interpretation, not a question of policy." Thus, he wrote, the Court had no authority to second-guess Congress or to decide whether the Ohio supplemental procedure was the best method for the state to police its voting rolls. He concluded that "The only question before us is whether it violates federal law. It does not."[13]

---

[12]*Husted v. A. Philip Randolph Institute* decision, page 20.
[13]Ibid., page 21.

In dissent, Justice Stephen Breyer quoted a Senate report on the NVRA: "The purpose of our election process is not to test the fortitude and determination of the voter, but to discern the will of the majority."[14] He argued that the worthy goal in having accurate voting lists did not justify imposing obstacles that would prevent eligible voters from participating.

Breyer marshaled evidence to show that Ohio sent out 1.5 million notices (roughly one-fifth of the state's eligible voters) despite the fact that on average less than five percent of Americans move to another county each year. Less than twenty percent of those receiving notices replied to the state. Of those, four times as many people responded that Ohio had made an error and they had not in fact moved. The vast majority, over one million, never responded. Justice Breyer considered this no more than the "the human tendency not to send back cards received in the mail."[15] The dissent argued that the Ohio Supplemental Process does in fact and effect rely on the failure to vote to purge voter rolls and the additional requirement of responding to a mailed notice does not mitigate violation of the National Voting Registration Act.

In a separate dissent, Justice Sonia Sotomayor focused on the broader consequences. She said that the Ohio law was part of a number of "concerted state efforts to prevent minorities from voting and to undermine the efficacy of their votes." She lamented that this was a long-standing and "unfortunate feature of our country's history."[16]

The *Husted* decision is bound to have significant consequences. According to Adam Liptak: "On one level, the decision sought to make sense of tangled statutory language. But it was also a vivid reminder that measures placing obstacles between people seeking to vote and their ability to cast ballots—including cutbacks on early voting, elimination of same-day registration and tough voter ID laws—present dueling visions of democracy."[17]

---

[14]*Husted* Breyer dissent, page 2.

[15]Ibid., page 13.

[16]*Husted* Sotomayor dissent, page 1.

[17]Adam Liptak, "Supreme Court Upholds Ohio's Purge of Voting Rolls," *The New York Times*, 11 June 2018.

Some decisions of the Supreme Court have a limited effect; others have a lasting impact. *Husted* is a prime example of the latter and will serve as a "how-to" for other legislatures and an invitation for multiple states to try to construct their own versions or simply adapt the Ohio model.

5

Janus v. AFSCME on Mandatory Fees to Public Sector Unions

Brett Curry

The Supreme Court's decision in *Janus* marked the end of a six-year drama in three acts—and Justice Samuel Alito was in the director's chair throughout the production. In the first act, a majority of the Court declared in *Knox v. Service Employees International Union* in 2012 that the First Amendment bars public sector unions from levying special assessments without a member's consent.[1] Union leaders argued that if individuals had to consent to the fees, many would be "free-riders," gaining the benefits of the union actions without paying to support them. Justice Alito wrote that "acceptance of the free-rider argument as a justification for compelling nonmembers to pay a portion of union dues represents something of an anomaly—one that we have found to be justified by the interest in furthering 'labor peace.' But it is an anomaly nevertheless."[2] The jurisprudential "anomaly" Alito

---

[1] *Knox v. SEIU*, 567 U.S. 310 (2012).
[2] Ibid.

B. Curry (✉)
Georgia Southern University, Statesboro, Georgia

© The Author(s) 2019
D. Klein and M. Marietta (eds.), *SCOTUS 2018*,
https://doi.org/10.1007/978-3-030-11255-4_5

referenced was *Abood v. Detroit Board of Education*, a 1977 decision in which the Supreme Court upheld the ability of public sector unions to assess so-called "agency fees."[3] *Abood* represented a judicially created balance between "employee speech," on the one hand and "managerial interests," on the other: it permitted the collection of mandatory fees from non-union members (agency fees) for use in collective bargaining efforts, but prohibited their use for "political" or "ideological" purposes.[4]

The second act commenced two years after *Knox*, when Alito wrote for a 5-4 majority in *Harris v. Quinn*. Alito and his conservative colleagues drew a distinction between "full-fledged" and "partial" public employees (in that case, home healthcare workers), holding that the latter fell outside the scope of *Abood*, and rendered the collection of agency fees from them impermissible. But even as it decided the case on narrow grounds, Alito's opinion left no doubt as to the preferences he and his conservative colleagues had about the story's arc. As Justice Elena Kagan's dissent in *Harris* observed, "[r]eaders of today's decision will know that *Abood* does not rank on the majority's top-ten list of favorite precedents—and that the majority could not restrain itself from saying (and saying and saying) so."[5] A leading Supreme Court reporter called Alito's opinion "A Ruling Inviting a Plea to Overrule,"[6] and another observer concluded that Alito had rendered *Abood* "a ghoul, one of the walking dead."[7] Conservative legal forces took immediate note of the Court's invitation and began shepherding cases through the lower courts they hoped the Justices might use to kill *Abood*.[8]

---

[3] *Abood v. Detroit Board of Education*, 431 U.S. 209 (1977).

[4] *Janus* decision, page 3.

[5] *Harris v. Quinn*, 573 U.S. ___ (2014), Justice Kagan dissent, page 15.

[6] Lyle Denniston, "Opinion Analysis: A Ruling Inviting a Plea To Overrule" www.SCOTUSblog.com, 30 June 2014.

[7] John Eastman, "*Harris v. Quinn* Symposium: *Abood* and the Walking Dead" www.SCOTUSblog.com, 30 June 2014.

[8] Brianne J. Gorod, "Sam Alito: The Court's Most Consistent Conservative," 126 *The Yale Law Journal* 362–373 (2017).

The third and final act of the story seemed to be speeding toward its conclusion when *Friedrichs v. California Teachers Association* came to the Court for oral argument in January 2016.[9] Instead, Justice Antonin Scalia's sudden death the next month brought an intermission. The short-handed Court was deadlocked and upheld the lower court's pro-union ruling in a 4-4 decision. It would take a presidential election and the elevation of a ninth Justice to break the impasse, to determine which script—Alito's or Kagan's—would carry the day.

With Donald Trump's election and Neil Gorsuch's elevation to the High Court, few were surprised when *Janus v. AFSCME*, a case from the Seventh Circuit, was granted *certiorari* and scheduled for argument in early 2018.[10] Mark Janus was a child-support specialist with the Illinois Department of Healthcare and Family Services who refused to be a member of the union. A majority of employees in his unit voted to be represented by the American Federation of State, County, and Municipal Employees (AFSCME). As a consequence, under the Illinois Public Labor Relations Act, the state recognized AFSCME as the exclusive representative of all the unit's workers—even those who, like Janus, were not members themselves and might not wish for the union to advocate on their behalf. Under *Abood*, AFSCME could charge nonmembers such as Janus a limited fee to cover "activities that are 'germane to [the union's] duties as collective bargaining representative.'" In Janus's case, that fee amounted to $45 per month, or approximately 78% of full union dues.[11] Janus objected to paying this fee and argued that because public sector bargaining is inherently political, the state's requirement amounted to coerced political speech. Janus' position was that the line *Abood* had drawn between collective bargaining and subsidizing the political and ideological activities of unions was artificial and unworkable. He lost in the lower courts, with Judge Richard Posner authoring the panel's ruling applying the *Abood* precedent.

---

[9] *Friedrichs v. California Teachers Association* 578 U.S. ___ (2016).

[10] Note: granting *certiorari* ("SER-shee-o-RARE-ree") is the term for the Court accepting a case to be heard. The Justices only take the appeals they choose to and are under little obligation to hear any specific case appealed from a lower court. They follow what is called the Rule of Four: if four of the nine Justices choose to hear a case, it is granted *certiorari*.

[11] *Janus* decision, page 3.

Janus at the Court

Oral argument at the Supreme Court can offer prognosticators strong indications about where the Justices are leaning. But *Janus* was different. Since the eight Justices who heard *Friedrichs* were known to be evenly divided, all eyes turned to freshman Justice Neil Gorsuch. Many assumed that, as a conservative, Gorsuch would probably side with his right-of-center colleagues and vote to invalidate the agency fees in question. But Gorsuch asked no questions during the hour-long argument, making it impossible to divine his position for another four months. On June 27, 2018, when Chief Justice John Roberts announced that Justice Alito had authored the Court's opinion, the result was immediately clear: government workers like Mark Janus who did not wish to join unions could not be required to subsidize their collective bargaining. The 5-4 decision held that such compelled payments violate the First Amendment: "We conclude that this arrangement violates the free speech rights of nonmembers by compelling them to subsidize private speech on matters of substantial public concern."[12]

Alito's opinion observed that the *Janus* proceedings revealed several problems with attempts to separate collective bargaining from political or ideological activity. First, the state law at issue lacked detail as to just which expenditures were "chargeable" to nonmembers and which were not. Second, the majority noted Janus' concerns about the fiscal position of Illinois and said those were political in character. In Janus's view, AFSCME's "behavior in bargaining [did] not appreciate the current fiscal crises in Illinois," and the Court called this a policy issue of paramount importance.[13] Moreover, given the fungible nature of money, the fees nonmembers contribute to collective bargaining could indirectly be applied to political advocacy by freeing up a greater proportion of member dues for that purpose.[14]

---

[12]Ibid., page 1.

[13]Ibid., page 3.

[14]Megan McArdle, "Why You Should Care About the Supreme Court's *Janus* Decision," *The Washington Post*, 27 June 2018.

The Court's majority had cast its lot with Mark Janus and the First Amendment, but it could not ignore the reality of *Abood*. After all, the decision had been on the books for more than 40 years and while questions about the precedent's vitality had been raised by the majorities in *Knox* and *Harris*, important principles of *stare decisis* needed to be addressed. In the last third of his opinion, Alito turned to the question of whether the dictates of following precedent were sufficient to overcome the legal errors of the original decision. Weighing several considerations, he and the majority determined that *stare decisis* was not enough to save *Abood*.

Alito's discussion of *stare decisis* began by considering the quality of *Abood's* reasoning. In the majority's telling, *Abood* erroneously interpreted two earlier decisions and, in doing so, judged the issue of public sector agency fees under an improperly deferential standard for speech-related claims (given that clear First Amendment rights were invoked, the Court should have applied a strenuous standard of review to see if a constitutional violation had occurred). Alito went further, chastising the *Abood* majority for eliding important distinctions between collective bargaining in the public and private sectors. In addition to drawing on the Court's prior opinion in *Harris*, Alito pointed out that even *Abood's* defenders had implicitly acknowledged the weakness of the decision's reasoning by resting their defense of it on grounds that differed from the case's original justifications.

The opinion also cast doubt on the workability of *Abood*, calling the line it had demarcated between chargeable and nonchargeable expenses unacceptably vague.[15] The majority again invoked *Abood's* defenders, who at oral argument seemed to concede the need to revisit this line-drawing exercise to eliminate lingering vagueness. For the majority, the acknowledged inadequacy of a line that had taken 40 years to draw was powerful evidence that no amount of effort could make the distinction workable. Further, Alito said, subsequent legal and factual developments also worked against *Abood*. The opinion stressed that changes in pension liabilities and the prevalence of public sector unionism had given collective-bargaining greater political resonance than was true in 1977. More

---

[15]In Mark Janus's situation, the union considered the chargeable (nonpolitical) expenses to be 78% of the full union dues for all expenses.

to the point, he identified the anomalous nature of *Abood* when assessed against the Court's other leading free speech cases. Finally, Alito's opinion rejected the argument that so-called "reliance interests," or prior conformity with *Abood's* dictates, were sufficient to retain the decision.

Justice Elena Kagan's dissent, which she read portions of from the bench, took the majority to task. She flatly accused her colleagues of disregarding standard principles of *stare decisis* and said that "The majority has overruled *Abood* for no exceptional or special reason, but because it never liked the decision. It has overruled *Abood* because it wanted to."[16] She maintained *Abood* struck a reasonable balance between competing, valid considerations—individual First Amendment rights, on the one hand, and governmental regulation of the workforce, on the other—and that the majority had usurped principles of democratic governance in uprooting that understanding. She noted this would have far-reaching ramifications.

Her opinion was especially biting in excoriating the path by which the majority had overruled *Abood*. Harkening back to *Knox* and *Harris*, Kagan indicted the trail of criticism that the majority had assembled to undermine the decision: "Don't like a decision? Just throw some gratuitous criticisms into a couple of opinions and a few years later point to them as 'special justifications'" for overruling it. She referred to Alito's approach as "bootstrapping" and accused it of "mocking *stare decisis*."[17] But she could hardly deny it had been successful.

Janus, Speech, and the Constitution

In the narrowest sense, *Janus* was the culmination of an effort by the Court's conservative majority to vindicate the free speech rights of non-union members. But it also reflected the libertarianism that has come to characterize the Roberts Court's approach toward speech cases generally. One may, of course, reasonably interpret *Janus* as an anti-union decision. However, it should be noted that the approach taken some years earlier

---

[16]*Janus* Kagan dissent, page 27.
[17]Ibid., page 21.

by the Court in *Citizens United v. F.E.C.* relied on a similarly muscular view of the First Amendment's protection of speech to strike down limits on independent expenditures by corporations and unions for purposes of electioneering "communications."[18] From a constitutional standpoint, the commonality between the two cases for the majority was not unions per se, but skepticism toward governmental regulations burdening speech.

Regardless, the majority's decision in *Janus* prompted accusations from both the dissenters and a number of commentators that the Court had succeeded in "weaponizing the First Amendment, in a way that unleashes judges, now and in the future, to intervene in economic and regulatory policy."[19] Or, as Professor Louis Seidman put it, "Instead of providing a shield for the powerless," the First Amendment had become "a sword used by people at the apex of the American hierarchy of power."[20] In addition to joining Kagan's dissent, Justice Sonia Sotomayor wrote her own one-paragraph opinion in *Janus*. In 2011, Sotomayor had abandoned her more liberal colleagues and sided with the Court's conservatives to invalidate a Vermont law related to pharmaceutical marketing. In that case, the Court concluded "speech in aid of pharmaceutical marketing... is a form of expression."[21] Using that case as a springboard, the Supreme Court seemed increasingly amenable to First Amendment arguments that could facilitate deregulation. Sotomayor believed that the 2011 decision had been misapplied because, as Kagan reminded readers of *Janus*, "almost all economic and regulatory policy affects or touches speech."[22]

Critics of the Court's approach in *Janus* immediately pointed to another ruling—*NIFLA v. Becerra*—underscoring their concern with the Court's direction in compelled speech cases.[23] The day before announcing *Janus*, the same five Justices in that majority had ruled

---

[18]*Citizens United v. F.E.C.* 558 U.S. 310 (2010).

[19]*Janus* Kagan dissent, page 26.

[20]Adam Liptak, "How the Supreme Court Weaponized the First Amendment," *The New York Times*, 30 June 2018.

[21]*Sorrell v. IMS Health, Inc.*, 564 U.S. 552 (2011).

[22]*Janus* Kagan dissent, page 28.

[23]*National Institute of Family & Life Advocates (NIFLA) v. Becerra*, 585 U.S. ___ (2018).

against a California regulation requiring "crisis pregnancy centers"—licensed facilities opposed to abortion that promote alternatives such as adoption—to post notices informing women about the availability of state-provided abortion services. Justice Clarence Thomas' opinion found this to offend the First Amendment, because it effectively commandeered abortion opponents into expressing a message that was contrary to their views. Justice Stephen Breyer's dissent, like Kagan's in *Janus*, pointed to potential consequences of the majority's approach: "Because much, perhaps most, human behavior takes place through speech and because much, perhaps most, law regulates that speech in terms of its content, the majority's approach at the least threatens considerable litigation over the constitutional validity of much, perhaps most, government regulation."[24]

Libertarian supporters of the Court's work have embraced these free speech rulings, in part because of the belief that speech-based rationales are more palatable with the public. The Supreme Court has not been alone in its receptiveness to these sorts of arguments—a number of recent lower court decisions have also embraced speech-based challenges to regulation. For example, in 2013, the D.C. Circuit used a compelled speech framework to strike down a rule that required companies to post federal labor protections. It employed similar logic to find that the Food and Drug Administration could not compel cigarette manufacturers to display graphic warning labels on their products.[25]

Janus and the Country

The implications of *Janus* were not lost on the Supreme Court. Justice Alito's opinion acknowledged that the loss of revenue from nonmember payments would likely spawn "unpleasant transition costs" for unions and require them to adjust strategically.[26] *Janus'* impact was doubly

---

[24]*NIFLA* Breyer dissent, page 3.
[25]Haley Sweetland Edwards, "How the First Amendment Became a Tool for Deregulation," *Time Magazine*, 19 July 2018.
[26]*Janus* decision, page 47.

disappointing to unions because, in addition to invalidating the mandatory payment of agency fees, the Court imposed an additional hurdle—it required clear and affirmative consent before individuals could opt in, making nonpayment of fees the default choice for nonmembers. Kagan warned that the decision would lead to instability in thousands of contracts; just in New York City, she noted, 144 contracts with 97 unions would be affected.[27]

Although the full impact of *Janus* remains to be seen, it appears all but certain that public sector unions will lose members and funds in its wake. When *Janus* was announced, 22 states allowed unions to collect agency fees, and public sector unions in those states are likely to become smaller and poorer. One study has suggested that public sector unions could lose three million members and hundreds of millions of dollars, and the National Education Association alone has estimated that the decision could mean a loss of 200,000 members and $28 million in revenue.[28]

At the same time, the decision was hardly a bolt from the blue. National teacher unions had been preparing for a *Janus*-like ruling for years and, in many states, public sector unions have been on the defensive for some time. In fact, a handful of progressive states passed preemptive measures to counteract the decision's effects. As an example, in the interim between oral argument and the Court's decision in *Janus*, Governor Andrew Cuomo signed legislation in New York eliminating the statutory requirement that unions represent non-dues paying workers.[29]

Buoyed by the decision, conservatives have begun bringing lawsuits in efforts to retroactively recover the agency fees that *Janus* invalidated. It is uncertain what traction, if any, might develop on that front. There is some anecdotal evidence that the case has increased union cohesion, and internal organizing may be poised to create a more activist culture amongst union members. On the other hand, the decision's supporters

---

[27]*Janus* Kagan dissent, page 24.

[28]Noam Scheiber, "Labor Unions Will Be Smaller After Supreme Court Decision, but Maybe Not Weaker," *The New York Times*, 27 June 2018; Dana Goldstein and Erica L. Green, "What the Supreme Court's *Janus* Decision Means for Teacher Unions," *The New York Times*, 27 June 2018.

[29]Goldstein and Green.

suggested that any diminution in the power of unions that results from *Janus* might ultimately be beneficial for the public at large, limiting a source of union leverage during a time of resource strain on state and municipal budgets.

The Roman god Janus is typically depicted with two faces—one looking to the future and the other to the past. As with this archetype from classical antiquity, there is a duality present in the Supreme Court's decision of the same name. Looking backward, the decision signifies the Roberts Court's enthusiastic embrace of limits on coerced speech and its willingness to jettison a long-standing precedent to the contrary. With the benefit of hindsight, it seems evident that the Court was working methodically toward that goal. But what of the future? Has its coerced speech jurisprudence reached a zenith, or does it remain a work in progress? While it is impossible to know for sure, the most zealous free speech advocates will certainly press the Court to go further. As Justices Ginsburg and Kagan observed at oral argument in *Friedrichs*, the Court's coercive speech cases are certain to raise a litany of further questions. What potential implications surround the Court's approach when the logic of *Janus* is applied to other types of mandatory contributions that might be channeled toward arguably political purposes? Might these include student activities fees? Or other associational dues?[30] At this writing, the Justices are weighing whether to grant *certiorari* to a North Dakota case challenging the constitutionality of mandatory bar dues.[31] How it resolves that threshold decision and others like it will be telling about the Court's penchant for policing coerced speech in a post-Justice Kennedy world.

---

[30] *Friedrichs v. California Teachers Association*, argument transcript at 35.
[31] *Fleck v. Wetch*, 868 F.3d 652 (8th Circuit).

6

Masterpiece Cakeshop on Gay Rights Versus Religious Liberty

Stephen M. Engel

In constitutional debate on gay and lesbian rights, dignity is the catch-word.[1] However, dignity is *not* a word in the U.S. Constitution. While many constitutions written since World War II contain explicit guarantees that human dignity shall not be trampled upon—and in many countries, gay rights claims have been litigated under these dignity clauses—the U.S. Constitution does not.[2] Prior to the gay rights litigation of the last two decades, dignity was not a term often used in Supreme Court decisions. As one legal scholar has poignantly written, "American constitutional jurisprudence is always something of an outlier, and no less with respect to human dignity… uniquely in the world, the U.S. Supreme Court has always been much more comfortable

---

[1]In this chapter, I use the phrase "gay and lesbian rights" as opposed to LGBTQ rights because in its jurisprudence on the subject, the Supreme Court has not used the more inclusive acronym, but has referred more often to the rights of "gays and lesbians" or "gay persons."

[2]See Aharon Barak, *Human Dignity: The Constitutional Value and the Constitutional Right* (New York: Cambridge University Press, 2015).

S. M. Engel (✉)
Bates College, Lewiston, ME, USA

© The Author(s) 2019
D. Klein and M. Marietta (eds.), *SCOTUS 2018*,
https://doi.org/10.1007/978-3-030-11255-4_6

attaching dignity to inanimate things, such as states and courts and contracts, than to human beings."[3] Even as the Court has begun to recognize human dignity more frequently and consistently, that move may have hit a dead end in 2018.

The Case

In *Masterpiece Cakeshop, ltd. v. Colorado Civil Rights Commission*, a same-sex couple sought to hire a baker to design a wedding cake. The baker, citing religious objections to same-sex marriage, refused to do so. The case pits a First Amendment freedom of religious exercise claim against a Fourteenth Amendment equal protection claim. How are these two claims to be balanced? The majority ruling written by Justice Anthony Kennedy—and joined by six other Justices, with only Ginsburg and Sotomayor dissenting—reveals that dignity, as such, is a constitutional dead end. Because it is not textually grounded in the Constitution and because it has no long-standing legacy of precedent to lean upon, dignity offers no metric by which to balance competing interests. To put the matter bluntly: whose dignity matters more, the same-sex couple seeking to marry in just the way the Supreme Court has already affirmed or the religious believer whose conscience commands that he not participate in a ceremony that violates his faith?

The Turn to Dignity

Some legal analysts have contended that *Masterpiece Cakeshop* will have little impact because the majority ruling avoids the substantive question presented and instead focuses on principles of neutral procedure.[4] Others maintain that the baker's victory was a significant assertion

---

[3]Erin Daly, *Dignity Rights: Courts, Constitutions, and the Worth of the Human Person* (Philadelphia: University of Pennsylvania Press, 2013), page 71.

[4]Richard A. Epstein, *The Worst Form of Judicial Minimalism—Masterpiece Cakeshop Deserved a Full Vindication for Its Claims of Religious Liberty and Free Speech*, SCOTUSblog, 4 June 2018.

that state actors cannot disrespect an individual's religious liberty.[5] This chapter points to how these readings may follow, but it also contends that the Court's turn to dignity may be the very reason the ruling admits of so many possible interpretations and hardly resolves the question at stake.

While dignity, as a constitutional right, may be more developed in international law and in constitutional traditions from Europe and South Africa, it is not a new concept in U.S. constitutional jurisprudence. The term has appeared in Supreme Court rulings and dissents since at least *Skinner v. Oklahoma* (1942), where the Court considered state-mandated sterilization to violate dignity, and Justice Murphy's famous dissent in *Korematsu v. United States* (1944), where internment of U.S. citizens of Japanese decent was characterized as "destroy[ing] the dignity of the individual."[6] These early uses hardly amounted to a consistent doctrine with a clear definition; scholars have called the treatment of dignity in the U.S. constitutional tradition "episodic and underdeveloped," "tentative," and "fragmented."[7] As legal scholar Aharon Barak summarizes the trend of the Court, "The Justices point out that their decisions are an attempt to realize human dignity, but they do not explain what human dignity is, what it covers, and what are the elements that comprise it."[8] Nowhere has the term been more consistently invoked than in Justice Anthony Kennedy's gay rights rulings: *Romer, Lawrence, Windsor*, and *Obergefell*.[9] And, even in these cases, the term is never defined.

---

[5]Elizabeth Clark, *And the Winner Is ... Pluralism?* SCOTUSblog, 6 June 2018.

[6]*Skinner v. State of Oklahoma*, ex rel. Williamson, 316 U.S. 535 (1942) at 546; *Korematsu v. United States*, 323 U.S. 214 (1944) at 214.

[7]Vicki C. Jackson, "Constitutional Dialogue and Human Dignity: States and Transnational Constitutional Discourse," 65 *Montana Law Review* (2004), page 17; Neomi Rao, "On the Use and Abuse of Dignity in Constitutional Law," 14 *Columbia Journal of European Law* (Spring 2008), page 202; Barak (2015), page 206.

[8]Barak (2015), page 206.

[9]*Lawrence v. Texas*, 539 U.S. 558 (2003) ruled that criminalization of consensual same-sex intimacy between two adults violated the Fourteenth Amendment; *United States v. Windsor*, 570 U.S. 744 (2013) ruled that section 3 of the federal Defense of Marriage Act (DOMA) defining marriage as only between one and man and one woman violated the Fourteenth Amendment; and, *Obergefell v. Hodges*, 576 U.S. ___ (2015) ruled that state bans on same-sex marriage violated the Fourteenth Amendment.

In 2013, when writing for the majority in *Windsor*, Justice Kennedy stipulated that when the state recognizes marriage, it "confer[s] upon them a dignity and status of immense import."[10] He considered a state government's decision to recognize same-sex marriage as constituting "further protection and dignity to that bond," representing a determination that same-sex couples were "worthy of dignity in the community equal with all other marriages."[11] Marriages "enhance the dignity and integrity of the person," which DOMA denies.[12] The statute was invalid because "no legitimate purpose overcomes the purpose and effect to disparage and to injure those whom the State, by its marriage laws, sought to protect in personhood and dignity."[13]

On June 27, 2015, *The New York Times* ran the banner headline "EQUAL DIGNITY" across its front page. The phrase was taken from Justice Kennedy's ruling for the Supreme Court majority in *Obergefell v. Hodges*, which struck down state bans on same-sex marriage. By pursuing a right to marry, gays and lesbians "ask for equal dignity in the eyes of the law. The Constitution grants them that right."[14] Just as he had in *Lawrence* and *Windsor*, Kennedy premised *Obergefell* on dignity; for Kennedy, marriage "always has promised nobility and dignity to all persons, without regard to their station in life."[15] He defined state recognition of marriage as a "basic dignity."[16]

Ironically, Kennedy's reliance on dignity could be used to curb gay rights claims—particularly those that take expression of sexual identity beyond the conceptual bounds of the private bedroom, household, and family—precisely because the term remains so undefined. Who has a greater claim on dignity: the gay or lesbian individual who seeks to live free from prejudice or the religious believer who also seeks to live

---

[10] *United States v. Windsor*, 570 U.S. ___ (2013), page 18.
[11] Ibid., page 20.
[12] Ibid., page 22.
[13] Ibid., page 25.
[14] *Obergefell* decision, page 28.
[15] Ibid., page 3.
[16] Ibid., page 26.

free from prejudice? In short, the potential exists for litigants and judges *to pit distinct conceptions of dignity against one another.* *Masterpiece Cakeshop* provided an opportunity to grapple with where a dignity doctrine might lead.

How *Masterpiece* Avoided the Question It Was Asked

In *Masterpiece*, the dignity doctrine has seemed to have reached its limit. The facts of that case involve a same-sex couple, Charlie Craig and David Mullins, who sought the services of Jack Phillips, owner of Masterpiece Cakeshop, to create a wedding cake. This occurred in 2012 when same-sex marriage was not recognized in Colorado (before *Obergefell* recognized same-sex marriages throughout the nation), and so, the couple sought to wed in Massachusetts and then hold a reception for family and friends at home in Colorado. Phillips indicated that while he would sell them other baked goods, he could not bake them a custom wedding cake because same-sex marriage violated his deeply held Christian beliefs.

Craig and Mullins filed a claim against Masterpiece Cakeshop under the Colorado Anti-Discrimination Act (CADA), which prevents discrimination in public accommodations—defined as any "place of business engaged in any sales to the public"—based on a set of protected characteristics including sexual orientation. The Colorado Civil Rights Commission (CCRC) investigated the claim and found probable cause of discrimination. The alleged violation of CADA was then referred to the Office of Administrative Courts. An Administrative Law Judge found for Craig and Mullins. Phillips appealed to the CCRC, but the CCRC affirmed the ALJ's ruling. Phillips appealed to the Colorado Court of Appeals in 2015, but this court found for Craig and Mullins. The Colorado Supreme Court denied Phillips' request for review; Phillips appealed to the United States Supreme Court.

In their written brief to the Supreme Court, lawyers for Phillips argued that CADA interfered with Phillips' free religious expression, and that any statute that conflicted with this First Amendment right would have to survive strict scrutiny (the state can only restrict his right to religious exercise if there is a compelling government interest, and they can only do so through the least restrictive means available). They maintained that the CCRC's objectives to prevent discrimination, to enable equal access to public accommodations, and to maintain the same-sex couple's dignity did not meet the strict scrutiny threshold. They argued that custom cake baking constituted a form of free speech or expressive conduct.

The CCRC countered that CADA would survive strict scrutiny but that it need not be applied, as the law at issue affected *commercial conduct* and not speech. Jack Phillips violated the law not because he held certain beliefs, but because he refused to serve an entire class of persons who were a protected class as defined by CADA. Perhaps most significantly, *both sides claimed dignitary harm*; Phillips claimed that CADA harmed the dignity of religious believers, while Craig and Mullins maintained that the denial of services undermined the dignity afforded to gays and lesbians required by law.

Kennedy's decision for the majority of seven Justices *did not* engage the question of the level of scrutiny applied.[17] Nor did it rule on whether CADA violated the First Amendment rights to religious expression or to speech. But Kennedy did recognize the essential tension in the competing claims to rights in his summary of the question at hand:

> The case presents difficult questions as to the proper reconciliation of at least two principles. The first is the authority of a State and its governmental entities to protect the rights and dignity of gay persons who are, or wish to be, married but who face discrimination when they seek goods or services. The second is the right of all persons to exercise fundamental freedoms under the First Amendment.[18]

---

[17]Justice Kennedy's opinion for the Court was joined by Alito, Breyer, Kagan, Gorsuch, and Roberts; Kagan filed a separate concurrence joined by Breyer; Gorsuch wrote a concurrence joined by Alito; Thomas wrote a concurrence joined by Gorsuch; and Ginsburg wrote the single dissent joined by Sotomayor.

[18]*Masterpiece Cakeshop v. Colorado Civil Rights Commission*, 584 U.S. ___ (2018), pages 1–2.

At issue is how to balance the Constitution's requirement of equal treatment (in the Fourteenth Amendment) against the Constitution's requirement of free religious exercise and free expression (in the First Amendment). Rather than answering this question, Kennedy restated the quandary over and over again. He reaffirmed the dignity of gays and lesbians: "Our society has come to the recognition that gay persons and gay couples cannot be treated as social outcasts or as inferior in dignity and worth. For that reason the laws and the Constitution can, and in some instances must, protect them in the exercise of their civil rights."[19] This imperative must recognize, as Kennedy wrote in *Obergefell*, that "those who adhere to religious doctrines, may continue to advocate with utmost, sincere conviction that, by divine precepts, same-sex marriage should not be condoned. The First Amendment ensures that religious organizations and persons are given proper protection as they seek to teach the principles that are so fulfilling and so central to their lives and faiths, and to their own deep aspirations to continue the family structure they have long revered."[20] Consequently, Kennedy continued in *Masterpiece*: "the religious and philosophical objections to gay marriage are protected views and in some instances protected forms of expression."[21] Nevertheless, Kennedy contended that these religious objections cannot extend to rights in commerce: "it is a general rule that such objections do not allow business owners and other actors in the economy and in society to deny protected persons equal access to goods and services under a neutral and generally applicable public accommodations law."[22]

Throughout *Masterpiece Cakeshop*, Kennedy suggests that individual freedom cannot be translated into practices that would otherwise indignify or subject gays and lesbians to stigma. But, the U.S. Constitution contains no explicit textual guarantee that government authorities must treat persons with dignity or especially that individual citizens must treat each other equally or without discrimination.

---

[19]Ibid., page 9.
[20]*Obergefell v. Hodges* decision, page 27.
[21]*Masterpiece* decision, page 9.
[22]Ibid.

Of course, certain forms of discrimination in commerce are illegal. The 1964 Civil Rights Act, particularly Section II, bans discrimination in public accommodations on grounds of race, color, religion, or national origin. However, the Fourteenth Amendment's guarantee of equal protection is not the source of constitutional authority that supports that statute. Instead, the 1964 Civil Rights Act was upheld in *Heart of Atlanta Motel v. United States* (1964) as a legitimate exercise of the Congress's Commerce Clause authority.[23] According to that ruling, Congress could regulate citizen-to-citizen interactions not because it sought to maintain equality, but because it had responsibility for maintaining economic well-being. The ban on discrimination was not a moral position that the government could impose on citizen-to-citizen interaction even if it had the effect of correcting a moral wrong.[24] Congress could regulate private businesses not because it sought to promote racial equality, but because racial discrimination had a negative effect on interstate commerce.

As Kennedy worked through the substantive issue at stake and the balance of the two principles—dignity rights of LGBT citizens and religious rights of vendors—he seems to suggest that the balance would tip in favor of the same-sex couple. While a state could justifiably not compel a member of the clergy to officiate a same-sex wedding, a blanket exemption on the basis of free exercise of religion would go too far: "if that exception were not confined, then a long list of persons who provide goods and services for marriages and weddings might refuse to do so for gay persons, thus resulting in a community-wide stigma inconsistent with the history and dynamics of civil rights laws that ensure equal access to goods, services, and public accommodations."[25] This suggests that "any decision in favor of the baker would have to be sufficiently constrained, lest all purveyors of goods and services who object to gay marriages for moral and religious reasons in effect be allowed to

---

[23] *Heart of Atlanta Motel, Inc. v. United States*, 379 *U.S.* 241 (1964).
[24] Ibid., page 258.
[25] *Masterpiece* decision, page 10.

put up signs saying 'no goods or services will be sold if they will be used for gay marriages,' something that would impose a serious stigma on gay persons."[26]

Nevertheless, Kennedy did not reach the conclusion that would vindicate the couple's claim and uphold the state rulings that led to the Court's involvement. Instead, he identified a process failure on the part of the state government in failing to treat the baker's religious identity with the respect required by the Constitution. Hostility was allegedly evident in the following statement from a CCRC member: "if a businessman wants to do business in the state and he's got an issue with the—the law's impacting his personal belief system, he needs to look at being able to compromise."[27] That statement could simply be positing that the businessman must engage in the very balancing that Kennedy claimed that the Court must perform. However, Kennedy read the sentiment as hostile because of another statement offered at a later meeting:

> I would also like to reiterate what we said in the hearing or the last meeting. Freedom of religion and religion has been used to justify all kinds of discrimination throughout history, whether it be slavery, whether it be the holocaust, whether it be—I mean, we—we can list hundreds of situations where freedom of religion has been used to justify discrimination. And to me it is one of the most despicable pieces of rhetoric that people can use to—to use their religion to hurt others.[28]

The majority of Justices agreed that this statement illustrates bias because it called faith "despicable" and implied that the belief was insincere. However, one could also read the commissioner's comment as drawing attention to how religious beliefs have been used to justify a broad range of policies—ranging from slavery to bans on interracial sex and marriage to bans on same-sex intimacy—that would now be

---

[26]Ibid., page 12.
[27]Ibid., pages 12–13.
[28]Ibid., page 13.

understood as grounded in animus.[29] Can the observation of well-evidenced historical pattern be an indication of undue prejudice against a religious believer?

By focusing on the alleged procedural breakdown at the CCRC review, Kennedy avoided the substantive issue at stake. He did not (and perhaps could not) offer the balancing required. Perhaps this is because dignity does not easily admit of a metric that can provide such balancing. If everyone has an inherent dignity, then no one's dignity can be said to be more valued without fundamentally denying a principle of equality.[30] Kennedy reached for a process critique perhaps because his dignity jurisprudence has hit a substantive dead end. He ended the decision were he began it, by noting that eventually the Court will have to balance the issues to which Kennedy proved unwilling or unable: "The outcome of cases like this in other circumstances must await further elaboration in the courts, all in the context of recognizing that these disputes must be resolved with tolerance, without undue disrespect to sincere religious beliefs, and without subjecting gay persons to indignities when they seek goods and services in an open market."[31] Put differently, everyone has dignity and so the case could not be resolved by resorting to the idea of equal dignity. In this sense, *Masterpiece* seems to reveal the dead end of dignity when applied to rights in commerce.

---

[29]See William N. Eskridge, Jr., "Noah's Curse: How Religion Often Conflates Status, Belief, and Conduct to Resist Antidiscrimination Norms," 45 *Georgia Law Review* (2011); James M. Oleske, Jr., "The Evolution of Accommodation: Comparing the Unequal Treatment of Religious Objections to Interracial and Same-Sex Marriages," 50 *Harvard Civil Rights-Civil Liberties Law Review* (2015); Greg Johnson, "We've Heard This Before: The Legacy of Interracial Marriage Bans and the Implications for Today's Marriage Equality Debates," 34 *Vermont Law Review* (2009).

[30]On dignity as inherent in either the Christian or Kantian traditions, see Andrea Sangiovanni, *Humanity Without Dignity: Moral Equality, Respect, and Human Rights* (Cambridge: Harvard University Press, 2017), pages 27–60.

[31]*Masterpiece* decision, page 18.

Implications

Inherent in the majority's proceduralist decision is perhaps an unwillingness to tackle the substantive issue of whether a same-sex wedding is, indeed, a wedding or, put differently, the Court does not address whether the equal dignity that it affirmed in *Obergefell* must now, in fact, be recognized.

That the baker, Phillips, could claim that baking this cake would constitute an indignity toward him is premised not only on the idea that a wedding cake carries an explicit message, but also that a cake for a *same-sex* wedding carries a *distinct* message than a cake for a cross-sex marriage. By conceptualizing the cake as "a cake celebrating same-sex marriage" rather than just a wedding cake (as Justice Gorsuch does in his concurrence agreeing with Phillips), the same-sex couple is positioned as *lacking* equal dignity.[32] Their cake is for something different from a "real" wedding. Kagan denies this distinction; "it was simply a wedding cake—one that (like other standard wedding cakes) is suitable for use at same-sex and opposite weddings alike."[33] *Obergefell*, with its specific call that LGBTQ persons are entitled to the respect of equal dignity, decries the injustice inherent in the distinction.

Since *Masterpiece* does not answer the question it is asked, future cases will need to do so (as Kennedy himself points out in the closing paragraphs of his decision). Therefore, questions remain. First, what constitutes evidence of religious animus by the state; is the mere recognition of how religious doctrines have historically shaped oppression a form of animus toward the contemporary religious believer? Second, since religious expression is a fundamental right and LGBTQ status has never been deemed a suspect class, does that mean that when the two come into conflict, the balance will always tip toward the religious believer? Put more concretely, will a claim of religious belief protect other service providers and public accommodations like florists, artists, restaurants, catering venues, etc.? Could it be used to deny LGBTQ

---

[32]*Masterpiece Cakeshop*, Gorsuch concurrence, page 3.

[33]*Masterpiece Cakeshop*, Kagan concurrence, page 3.

individuals equal access to employment or housing? And, if religious belief becomes a shield in this regard—and we might turn to *Burwell v. Hobby Lobby* (2014) as a critical rivet in that emerging armor—then how can we realize Kennedy's position that LGBT persons not suffer indignity at the hands of religious believers?[34] Finally, how will partisan politics be affected by continuing to position religious believers and LGBTQ persons as opponents on these cultural-legal questions? Will the same cultural politics that emerged in the 1980s and 1990s acquire renewed resonance as Republicans side with religious believers; will LGBTQ individuals become or, indeed, remain primarily captured by the Democratic party?[35]

Conclusion

The decision in *Masterpiece Cakeshop* reveals the unwillingness of Justice Kennedy to carry out the implications of the constitutional tradition for which he has become almost singularly responsible. In *Masterpiece*, he repeatedly stipulates that gays and lesbians cannot be denied their dignity and that denial of services grounded in their sexual orientation would constitute an indignity. And yet, he avoids this conclusion by focusing on a procedural failure.

Perhaps the more troubling and immediate legacy of *Masterpiece* is that it may be misused as precedent to stand for far more than it does. While Phillips won the case, the decision resolved nothing. It did not stipulate, as much as some concurrences may have wished, that First Amendment freedoms of expression or religious exercise take priority over equal treatment guaranteed in the Fourteenth Amendment. It

---

[34]*Burwell v. Hobby Lobby*, 537 U.S. ___ (2014) ruled that closely held private corporations could be exempt from federal regulations if such regulations conflicted with their religious beliefs.

[35]On the long-standing opposition between the evangelical right and the LGBT movement, see Chris Bull and John Gallagher, *Perfect Enemies: The Religious Right, the Gay Movement, and the Politics of the 1990s* (New York: Crown, 1996); on vote capture of the LGBTQ movement by the Democratic Party, see Paul Frymer, *Uneasy Alliances: Race and Party Competition in America* (Princeton: Princeton University Press, 2010).

simply ruled that an administrative body behaved badly in demeaning sincerely held religious belief, and that it should avoid such behavior in the future. Nevertheless, given the increasing presence of conservative jurists throughout the federal judiciary, it could come to stand for the much broader idea that the First Amendment provides insulation or protection against a command of equal treatment.[36] In light of this possibility, perhaps we need to interrogate more deeply why we are willing to read the First Amendment so broadly and yet read the commands of the Fourteenth Amendment so narrowly.

---

[36]Peter Baker, "A Conservative Court Push Decades in the Making, With Effects for Decades to Come," *The New York Times*, 9 July 2018.

7

Trump v. Hawaii on the Travel Ban

Anthony A. Peacock

Trump v. Hawaii was one of the most closely watched decisions of the term. The reason was that the case involved an issue that many political experts believe won Donald Trump the 2016 presidential election: immigration. While a candidate, President Trump had made enforcement of America's borders a central platform of his candidacy. And that enforcement did not just stop at building a wall on the Mexican border. It also involved scrutiny of who would be allowed into the United States from countries that the President as well as prior administrations and Congresses had deemed a threat to national security.

On September 24, 2017, President Trump issued Proclamation No. 9645. That order sought more vigorous vetting procedures for foreign nationals traveling to the United States from countries that had failed to share adequate information with the United States or otherwise presented a national security threat. After a 50-day period of review against a baseline measure for national security compliance by the Department of Homeland Security, the State Department, and intelligence agencies, eight countries were determined to be deficient in meeting minimum

A. A. Peacock (✉)
Political Science Department, Utah State University, Logan, UT, USA

© The Author(s) 2019
D. Klein and M. Marietta (eds.), *SCOTUS 2018*,
https://doi.org/10.1007/978-3-030-11255-4_7

national security standards: Chad, Iran, Iraq, Libya, North Korea, Syria, Venezuela, and Yemen. Later, Iraq and Chad would be removed from this list while Somalia would be added.

As had been the case with two earlier executive orders involving travel restrictions from President Trump, Proclamation No. 9645 was immediately challenged in court. The plaintiffs were the state of Hawaii, three individuals whose relatives abroad had been affected by the entry suspension, and the Muslim Association of Hawaii. The plaintiffs claimed that the Proclamation violated provisions of the Immigration and Nationality Act (INA) as well as the Establishment Clause of the First Amendment.

The outcome in this third case was the same as it had been in the first two cases: a district court judge imposed a nationwide preliminary injunction against the order. The Ninth Circuit Court of Appeals affirmed the lower courts' order, finding that the Proclamation violated two provisions of the INA: Section 1182(f), authorizing the President to "suspend the entry of all aliens or any class of aliens" whenever he found that their entry "would be detrimental to the interests of the United States"; and Section 1152(a)(1)(A), which provided that "no person shall … be discriminated against in the issuance of any immigrant visa because of the person's race, sex, nationality, place of birth, or place of residence." The plaintiffs' Establishment Clause claim was not addressed by the Ninth Circuit.

When the case arrived before the U.S. Supreme Court, it was reversed on all counts. What was important about *Trump* was not only the Court's rejection of the lower court's interpretation of the INA, but its reaffirmation of executive authority in the area of national security. Contrary to a number of recent Court decisions, *Trump* seemed to herald the return of the national security Constitution. That understanding of the Constitution left little, if any, room for judicial intervention into national security questions. The courts, as an earlier line of Supreme Court jurisprudence affirmed, had neither the constitutional authority nor the institutional capacity to decide issues like those at play with the Proclamation. According to the majority, to allow the judiciary to intervene would be dangerous to national security. Both the plain meaning of the INA and the theory of executive responsibility under the Constitution counseled against the plaintiffs' claims and the ruling of the Ninth Circuit.

Chief Justice John Roberts wrote the Court's opinion, joined by Justices Anthony Kennedy, Clarence Thomas, Samuel Alito, and Neil Gorsuch. Justice Kennedy and Justice Thomas also wrote separate concurring opinions. Justice Breyer wrote a dissenting opinion, joined by Justice Elena Kagan, and Justice Sotomayor wrote an additional dissenting opinion, joined by Justice Ruth Bader Ginsburg. The deeply divided opinions offer conflicting visions of American constitutionalism, with broad implications for the breadth of executive power and the politics of the Trump era.

The Court's Opinion

Reversing the preliminary injunction as "an abuse of discretion,"[1] the Court suggested that the lower court's injunction against the travel ban was clearly in error. It began with a misconstruction of the INA. Contrary to what the lower courts had proposed, the majority of Justices found that the INA clearly gave President Trump the authority to issue the Proclamation. There were numerous grounds on which aliens abroad could be held inadmissible to the United States or ineligible for a visa: health-related grounds, criminal history, terrorist activities, and foreign policy grounds. Moreover, Section 1182 of the INA granted the President broad discretion to prohibit entry into the United States on the grounds that admission would be "detrimental" to the national interest. The discretion contemplated by Congress was excessively broad.

The Court further rejected the plaintiffs' contention that the Proclamation was based on inadequate evidence. At 12 pages long, the Proclamation was more detailed than any prior presidential order issued under Section 1182(f). It outlined at length the process as well as the agency evaluations and recommendations underlying the travel

---

[1] *Trump v. Hawaii* decision, page 38.

restrictions. By contrast, a 1996 proclamation by President Bill Clinton had explained in *one sentence* why it was necessary to suspend Sudanese government officials and military personnel from the United States for reasons of foreign policy. In 1981, President Ronald Reagan had similarly explained in a mere five sentences why it was necessary to suspend the illegal migration of a large number of undocumented aliens by sea into America's southeastern states. President Trump also did not have to place any time limit on the suspension order as the plaintiffs had asserted—none of the 43 previous suspension orders issued by other administrations had included any specific end dates. Chief Justice Roberts also pointed out that the Proclamation was limited in its effect. Lawful permanent residents were exempted from it, case-by-case waivers could be granted under specified circumstances, and the DHS had to continually assess countries' compliance with the Proclamation and report to the President every 180 days on whether restrictions should be continued or modified. Additionally, the Proclamation did not interfere with the visa waiver program that allowed travelers from 38 countries that had a rigorous security relationship with the United States from coming to the country on a short-term basis.

The Court's dispute with the plaintiffs, the lower courts, and the dissenters did not end with the interpretation of the text of the INA. The most significant controversy in the case was over the role of the President in what I have called the national security Constitution.[2] As far as the majority was concerned, the Constitution placed the primary responsibility for keeping the nation safe in the hands of the political branches of government: the Congress and the President. As Chief Justice Roberts wrote: "For more than a century, this Court has recognized that the admission and exclusion of foreign nationals

---

[2] By national security Constitution, I mean two things. First, the primacy the Founders placed on national security in the Constitution; that national security was the most important object the Constitution was to fulfill. Second, responsibility for the national security Constitution was placed in the hands of the President and Congress, not the judiciary. As two constitutional law scholars summarizing the war and foreign affairs powers the Constitution expressly grants to each branch of the federal government conclude: "What is most striking is the complete absence of the judiciary." Ralph A. Rossum and G. Alan Tarr, *American Constitutional Law: The Structure of Government, Vol. I*, 10th ed. (Boulder, CO: Westview Press, 2017), page 204.

is a 'fundamental sovereign attribute exercised by the Government's political departments largely immune from judicial control.'"[3] The power to decide national security issues had to follow the responsibility for carrying out national security policy. That responsibility lay with the President and Congress, not the judiciary. Roberts cautioned that "'judicial inquiry into the national-security realm raises concerns for the separation of powers' by intruding on the President's constitutional responsibilities in the area of foreign affairs."[4] Moreover, "'when it comes to collecting evidence and drawing inferences' on questions of national security, 'the lack of competence on the part of the courts is marked.'"[5]

For reasons of law and of institutional capacity, the judiciary has little, if any, role to play in national security decision-making. That includes immigration policy, particularly policy implemented with a view to keeping the nation safe. Roberts concluded the majority opinion by paraphrasing with approval from *Mathews v. Diaz* (1976): "'Any rule of constitutional law that would inhibit the flexibility' of the President 'to respond to changing world conditions should be adopted only with the greatest caution,' and our inquiry into matters of entry and national security is highly constrained."[6] It was unclear following this statement whether the Court would permit *any* form of review, but it immediately qualified that "the Government" *itself* had proposed that inquiry beyond the "facial neutrality of the order" might "be appropriate." Accordingly, Roberts proclaimed that "For our purposes today, we assume that we may look behind the face of the Proclamation to the extent of applying rational basis review."[7] Robert's qualification "for our purposes today" raised the specter that perhaps in future, where

---

[3] *Trump v. Hawaii* decision, page 30, citing *Fiallo v. Bell*, 430 U.S. 787 at 792 (1977).

[4] Ibid., page 31, citing *Ziglar v. Abbasi*, 582 U.S. ___ (2017) (opinion at 19).

[5] Ibid., pages 31–32, citing *Holder v. Humanitarian Law Project*, 561 U.S. 1 at 34 (2010).

[6] Ibid., page 32.

[7] Ibid. In rational basis review, the Court simply asks if a law or order, like the Proclamation, is rationally related to a legitimate government objective (in this case national security); if the answer is Yes, the order is constitutional. The party challenging the order has the burden of proving that it has no rational basis.

the executive branch was not prepared to allow any inquiry beyond the facial neutrality of an order, that the Court may not permit such a review to take place. In any event, the rational basis review required only that the government's stated objective of protecting the country and improving vetting processes be plausibly related to the entry policy. The Court determined it clearly was.

The Dissenters Respond

The dissenters emphatically disagreed. According to Justice Breyer, the key point of contention between the members of the Court centered on whether or to what extent anti-Muslim animus formed the basis of the Proclamation. If such animus did motivate the order, it would violate both the INA and the First Amendment. Examining the system of exemptions and waivers allowed under the auspices of the Proclamation, Justice Breyer determined that the Trump Administration was in fact disingenuous in describing the true intent of the entry restrictions. No executive guidance following the Proclamation had been issued as promised, the number of waivers granted were too small, and other data suggested that the Administration was restricting entry from the listed countries under fraudulent pretenses. For example, 15,000 refugees from Syria had been admitted to the United States in 2016; although the Proclamation did not apply specifically to refugees or asylum seekers, only 13 had arrived since January 2018. Similarly, only a small number of student visas had been issued for students from Iran, Libya, and Yemen. None had been issued to students from Somalia. "Declarations, anecdotal evidence, facts, and numbers taken from *amicus* briefs are not judicial factfindings," Breyer admitted. "The Government has not had an opportunity to respond, and a court has not had an opportunity to decide." Nevertheless, "given the importance of the decision in this case, the need for assurance that the Proclamation does not rest upon a 'Muslim Ban,' and the assistance in deciding the issue that answers to the 'exemption and waiver' questions may provide," Justice Breyer was prepared to return the case to the district court and to "leave the injunction in effect while the matter is litigated."[8]

Justice Sotomayor's dissent was even more emphatic than Breyer's. It began by cataloguing a host of statements made by the President before and after the election of 2016, which Sotomayor contended were anti-Muslim. Although the majority had summarized many of these same statements as well as additional background events over the course of a couple of pages in its opinion, they did "not tell even half the story" according to Sotomayor.[9] Reviewing the evidence, Sotomayor concluded that "none of the features of the Proclamation highlighted by the majority supports the Government's claim that the Proclamation is genuinely and primarily rooted in a legitimate national-security interest. What the unrebutted evidence actually shows is that a reasonable observer would conclude, quite easily, that the primary purpose and function of the Proclamation is to disfavor Islam by banning Muslims from entering our country."[10] For Sotomayor, the Proclamation clearly violated the Establishment Clause's promise of religious neutrality.

The majority had contended that the First Amendment considerations implicated by the Establishment Clause claim had to be qualified because what was at issue was a matter of national security. As noted above, this required deference to the political branches. Justice Sotomayor would have none of it. "In holding that the First Amendment gives way to an executive policy that a reasonable observer would view as motivated by animus against Muslims, the majority opinion upends this Court's precedent, repeats tragic mistakes of the past, and denies countless individuals the fundamental right of religious liberty. Just weeks ago, the Court rendered its decision in *Masterpiece Cakeshop…* which applied the bedrock principles of religious neutrality and tolerance in considering a First Amendment challenge to government action."[11]

---

[8]*Trump v. Hawaii* Justice Breyer dissent, page 8.

[9]*Trump v. Hawaii* Justice Sotomayor dissent, page 4.

[10]Ibid., page 23.

[11]Ibid., page 25.

Constitutional and Political Implications

Masterpiece was an odd authority for Sotomayor to cite here since she dissented in the case. She was only one of two Justices to do so. The seven other members of the Court, including more liberal members Justices Breyer and Kagan, found blatant discrimination by the Colorado Civil Rights Commission against Jack Phillips, a baker who had opposed making a cake for a same-sex couple's marriage on grounds of his Christian faith. The Court in *Masterpiece* had chastised the Commission (the respondent on appeal) for effectively dissing Phillip's Christian faith and free exercise of religion rights in preference for the claims of the same-sex couple that brought the action against Phillips before the Commission. Sotomayor evinced little, if any, sympathy for Phillip's claims of religious freedom.

Masterpiece exemplified the problem as the Court saw it with Justice Sotomayor's approach to the issues in *Trump*: the problem of political partisanship. Sotomayor was sympathetic to the claims of Muslims in *Trump*, but not sympathetic to the claims of a devout Christian in *Masterpiece*. The Court in *Trump* had criticized Sotomayor's "reasonable observer" standard because it was not only contrary to multiple, long-standing precedents but invited the partisan interpretation of the case law and evidence. What was "reasonable" to Justices Sotomayor and Ginsburg was anything but to the Court. As "perplexing" as the dissent found the majority's use of the rational basis standard of review, the majority maintained that it was nowhere near as problematic as "the dissent's assumption that courts should review immigration policies, diplomatic sanctions, and military actions under the de novo 'reasonable observer' inquiry applicable to cases involving holiday displays and graduation ceremonies.... The dissent can cite no authority for its proposition that the more free-ranging inquiry it proposes is appropriate in the national security and foreign affairs context."[12] Sotomayor conceded that the Court had "not confronted the precise situation at hand" in the past, but that even if there was "no prior case directly on

---

[12] *Trump v. Hawaii* decision, page 32 note 5.

point," it was clear from earlier precedent "that '[w]hatever power the United States Constitution envisions for the Executive' in the context of national security and foreign affairs, 'it most assuredly envisions a role for all three branches when individual liberties are at stake.'"[13]

The case Sotomayor cited here was *Hamdi v. Rumsfeld* (2004), the first of four cases decided between 2004 and 2008 in which the Court ruled against the Bush Administration and Congress in disputes over detainees in the War on Terror.[14] Like *Trump*, these decisions involved foreign policy and national security. Unlike *Trump*, the Court did not hesitate to intervene in national security decision-making, effectively displacing the political branches of government as the final authority for national security policy.

Trump seems to signal a return to a more deferential posture from the Court, one that accorded with long-standing precedent prior to *Hamdi*. Chief Justice Roberts chastised the plaintiffs and the dissenters in *Trump* for presuming that the Court could substitute its own judgment for that of the Executive's on matters like immigration and national security policy; "we cannot substitute our own assessment," Roberts proclaimed, "for the Executive's predictive judgments on such matters, all of which 'are delicate, complex, and involve large elements of prophecy.'" Roberts here was quoting from the Court's long-standing precedent, *Chicago & Southern Airlines, Inc. v. Waterman S.S. Corp* (1948). Justice Thomas had cited this same case in his dissent in *Hamdi*. There Thomas quoted Justice Robert Jackson's opinion on behalf of the Court in *Waterman* that decisions over foreign policy "are wholly confided by our Constitution to the political departments of government, Executive and Legislative." Such decisions "are and should be undertaken only by those directly responsible to the people whose welfare they advance or imperil. They are decisions of a kind for which the Judiciary has neither aptitude, facilities, nor responsibility and which has long been held to belong in the domain of political power not subject to judicial intrusion

---

[13] *Trump v. Hawaii* Justice Sotomayor dissent, pages 15–16 note 6.

[14] The other three cases were *Rasul v. Bush*, 542 U.S. 466 (2004), *Hamdan v. Rumsfeld*, 548 U.S. 557 (2006), and *Boumediene v. Bush*, 553 U.S. 723 (2008).

or inquiry."[15] With neither the aptitude nor responsibility to the people for foreign policy decisions, the Court had for decades recognized that foreign policy was a political question best left to the political branches to decide. The judiciary would be subordinate to the President in such decision-making—at least until *Hamdi*.

Justice Kennedy, who joined the plurality in *Hamdi*, joined the Court's more conservative members in *Trump*. Although his concurring opinion left open the possibility of the lower courts finding animus in President Trump's Proclamation, he again emphasized "the substantial deference that is and must be accorded to the Executive in the conduct of foreign affairs."[16]

Justice Thomas' concurring opinion would have gone even further by simply eliminating the possibility of any challenges like the plaintiffs' altogether. Not only did Section 1182(f) of the INA "not set forth any judicially enforceable limits that constrain the President," in his view, the Congress could *not* have done so because "the President has *inherent* authority to exclude aliens from the country."[17] In addition, there was no First Amendment claim available to the plaintiffs because such claims are not available to aliens abroad. Thomas also wanted to limit nationwide or universal injunctions of the sort the lower courts had imposed in *Trump* because such injunctions appeared to be an abuse of judicial power. Thomas argued that nationwide injunctions from district courts were a relatively new development and undermined the legal process by preventing decisions from percolating through the federal judicial system. In addition, they encouraged forum shopping. Plaintiffs challenging the Trump Administration's immigration policies could simply seek out judges in deep blue states who would be amenable to blocking the Administration's immigration orders nationwide. Although the *Trump* Court did not take up the issue of universal injunctions, Justice Thomas maintained that it would

---

[15] *Chicago & Southern Airlines*, 333 U.S. at 111, cited in *Hamdi v. Rumsfeld*, 542 U.S. 507 at 582, Thomas dissent.

[16] *Trump v. Hawaii* Justice Kennedy concurrence, page 1.

[17] *Trump v. Hawaii* Justice Thomas concurrence, page 1 (emphasis in original).

be duty bound to do so in future should federal courts continue to issue them.[18]

As if to accentuate this issue, on November 19, 2018 (five months after *Trump* was announced), a federal district court judge in San Francisco, Jon S. Tigar, issued a nationwide restraining order against President Trump's November 9, 2018 proclamation that only migrants applying for asylum at a legal port of entry to the United States would be processed. Trump subsequently lambasted Tigar as an "Obama judge." Chief Justice Roberts, in a rare statement to the Associated Press, responded that, "We do not have Obama judges or Trump judges, Bush judges or Clinton judges. What we have is an extraordinary group of dedicated judges doing their level best to do equal right to those appearing before them."[19] Responding to Roberts, Trump contended that the Chief Justice was wrong about the lack of political bias of many judges and went on to describe the Ninth Circuit Court of Appeals, based in San Francisco, as "a complete and total disaster."[20]

Like this more recent dispute over the question of migrants seeking asylum in the United States, the split in *Trump* reflected the broader political divisions within the country. The more conservative members of the Court supported President Trump in his attempts to provide security through new, more restrictive immigration policies. The more liberal members opposed these policies. The more conservative members of the Court tried to rein in judicial policy-making in national security. The more liberal members were happy to have the judiciary step in and constrain the President's discretion on these issues. With the shift in the composition of the Court from Justice Kennedy to Justice Kavanaugh, the trend may well continue toward greater judicial deference to national security.

But how far will that go? Another noteworthy aspect of the *Trump* decision was that the Court took the rather unusual step of overruling

---

[18]Ibid., page 10.

[19]Mark Sherman, "Roberts, Trump Spar in Extraordinary Scrap Over Judges," Associated Press, 21 November 2018.

[20]Quoted in "No Holiday from Trump Bashing Court," (Associated Press) *Salt Lake Tribune*, 23 November 2018.

Korematsu v. United States (1944). That case involved a challenge to an order allowing the government to hold persons of Japanese ancestry in internment camps during World War II. The Court's discussion of *Korematsu* in its ruling on *Trump* was unusual because as it acknowledged, "*Korematsu* has nothing to do with this case."[21] Nevertheless, since Justice Sotomayor's dissent had raised the issue of *Korematsu*, likening it to the facts in *Trump*, Chief Justice Roberts took "the opportunity to make express what is already obvious: *Korematsu* was gravely wrong the day it was decided, has been overruled in the court of history, and—to be clear—'has no place in law under the Constitution.'"[22]

Roberts was quoting from Justice Robert Jackson's dissenting opinion in *Korematsu*. That was an interesting choice to cite because Jackson emphasized in *Korematsu*, as he would four years later in *Waterman*, that the judiciary was in no position to second-guess the executive or the military on questions of national security. When it came to the military, "the paramount consideration is that its measures be successful, rather than legal. The armed services must protect a society, not merely its Constitution."[23]

Unlike the famous dissent by Justice Murphy, which denounced the Japanese internment in the strongest terms as the "legalization of racism," Justice Jackson seemed to suggest in *Korematsu* that the Court should never have taken the case on in the first place, because "in the very nature of things, military decisions are not susceptible of intelligent judicial appraisal."[24] As he concluded, if the Court hears the case and "a judicial opinion rationalizes such an order to show that it conforms to the Constitution" the Court "has validated the principle of racial discrimination in criminal procedure and of transplanting American citizens. The principle then lies about like a loaded weapon ready for the hand of any authority that can bring forward a plausible claim."[25]

---

[21] *Trump v. Hawaii* decision, page 38.

[22] *Trump v. Hawaii* decision, page 38, quoting *Korematsu v. United States* 323 U.S. 214 at 248, Justice Jackson dissent.

[23] *Korematsu* Justice Jackson dissent at 244.

[24] Ibid., Justice Murphy dissent at 242, Justice Jackson dissent at 245.

[25] Ibid., at 246.

Did Chief Justice Roberts' citation of Justice Jackson in *Korematsu* affirm the primacy of national security and the principle that the judiciary has no business second-guessing the President on questions of military necessity, until the point that the government engages in racial classifications that have "no place in law under the Constitution"? Roberts clarified further regarding *Korematsu* that "the forcible relocation of U.S. citizens to concentration camps, solely and explicitly on the basis of race, is objectively unlawful and outside the scope of Presidential authority."[26] Apparently, there *are* limits to what government can do in the name of national security, at least when bald race classifications were involved. But how far does this limit go? Short of large-scale imprisonment based on race, where is the limit of the principle that the executive can authorize whatever is deemed necessary to achieve military success, as Justice Jackson in both *Korematsu* and *Waterman* seems to propose? Roberts' opinion was by no means clear on any of these issues, and the brief discussion of *Korematsu* seemed to raise as many questions as it purported to answer.

---

[26] *Trump v. Hawaii*, page 38.

8

Wayfair on Internet Taxation

Morgan Marietta

My couch seems too comfortable to have constitutional significance. My wife and I bought it a few months ago from an Internet firm called Wayfair. We didn't pay sales tax because we live in New Hampshire, but if we still lived in Massachusetts and paid the tax, I wouldn't have thought much about it. But Wayfair doesn't think that this form of taxation is constitutionally permissible and I read *Wayfair* sitting on my Wayfair couch. Wayfair provided me a pleasant place to read the decision that ruled against them, grounded in a persuasive description of the new social facts of the Internet. But not everyone is persuaded. The case not only raises questions of great significance for the U.S. economy, but also addresses how the Court should deal with questions of the shifting social facts of our society.

M. Marietta (✉)
Department of Political Science, University of Massachusetts Lowell, Lowell, MA, USA

© The Author(s) 2019
D. Klein and M. Marietta (eds.), *SCOTUS 2018*,
https://doi.org/10.1007/978-3-030-11255-4_8

The Case

South Dakota v. Wayfair, Inc. was decided 5 to 4. Kennedy wrote the Court's decision, joined by Alito, Ginsburg, Gorsuch, and Thomas. Chief Justice Roberts dissented, joined by Breyer, Kagan, and Sotomayor. These somewhat unusual coalitions reflect the nature of the dispute: *Wayfair* is more about how the Court deals with social facts than constitutional principles, leading to strange bedfellows regarding Wayfair's furniture.

The case is about the constitutionality of taxation, specifically the power of a state to levy sales tax on a company that only does business with the state's citizens over the Internet, with no physical presence within the boundaries of the state. The suit focuses on South Dakota, but the decision notes that "forty-one States, two Territories, and the District of Columbia now ask this Court" to uphold South Dakota's position.[1] The economic meaning of the outcome is expansive. According to the *Stanford Law Review*, "the world of internet commerce was shaken to its foundations" by the decision.[2] The day after the decision was announced, business and tech media outlets weighed in on their perceptions of its meaning: "Supreme Court's Internet Sales Tax Ruling May Be a Nightmare for Small Businesses" was the headline at *The Verge*, an online tech magazine; "The end result of the ruling will be an increase in tax revenue for states and higher operating costs for internet sales companies, which will inevitably translate into higher costs for consumers" said MarketWatch.com; The *Wall Street Journal* called the decision "a milestone marking e-commerce's treatment as a mature player in a marketplace no longer defined by trips to the corner store or the shopping mall."[3] The editorial board of the *Journal* described it the day it was announced as "a ruling that liberates state and local politicians to tax the internet nationwide with

---

[1] *Wayfair* decision, page 16.

[2] Brian Galle, "Keep *Quill*, Keep the Dormant Commerce Clause," *Stanford Law Review*, March 2018.

[3] *The Verge*, 22 June 2018; MarketWatch.com, Paul Graney, 22 June 2018; *Wall Street Journal*, Jess Bravin and Brent Kendall, 22 June 2018.

abandon."[4] Internet sales have grown considerably in the last decade and are now massive. Wayfair alone had net revenues of $4.7 billion in 2017. The South Dakota Department of Revenue estimates potential tax revenues for the state rising to $48–$58 million each year, a very large amount of money for states like South Dakota that have no income tax and rely on alternative sources of revenue. But a state's need for funding does not make its actions constitutional, even if South Dakota asserts that "an emergency is hereby declared to exist," as they did in the state law enacted in 2016.[5]

One way to describe any objection that a government action is unconstitutional is to focus on what is being said about *powers* and *rights*: Does the government have the power, and does the government's action violate a right? Generally speaking, for any action to be constitutional, the answers must be *Yes* and *No*. The wrong answer to either question creates a constitutional violation. In *Wayfair*, there is no claim of a citizen right, as there is no recognized right against taxation. There are *limits* to taxation, as in the prohibitions against certain forms of taxation in the original Constitution, followed by the expansion of the government power to tax in the Sixteenth Amendment, specifically allowing for income taxes on individuals. In addition to the neutral search for government revenue—we must pay for roads and armies—any form of taxation has consequences for society and creates incentives for individuals. Any specific incentive could be unintentional or deeply intended by a legislature, but taxation is a constitutional power of government unless it crosses the line into coercion that violates a specific right. In the South Dakota case, no one seriously argues that a state cannot tax its citizens when they buy something: states have this power and individuals have no right against it. But *do states have the power to tax companies that reside in other states and have no physical presence in the taxing state?* There is no constitutional right of citizens of South Dakota to not be taxed when they buy something online that will be shipped from South Carolina, but does South Dakota have the *power* to lay that tax?

---

[4]"Springtime for Internet Taxers," *Wall Street Journal*, 21 June 2018.
[5]*Wayfair* decision, page 3.

The Interstate Commerce Clause in Reverse

The first paragraph of the majority decision states that the ruling "turns on a proper interpretation of the Commerce Clause."[6] The first sentence of the dissent clarifies that it is the *Dormant* Commerce Clause that is really at issue. This constitutional concept is also known as the *Negative* Commerce Clause. If the national government has control over *interstate* commerce (the power to "regulate commerce... among the several states"), then individual states *cannot* have this power and therefore are forbidden from doing anything that substantially interferes with interstate trade. States have the clear power to regulate *local* trade conditions for the safety or health of their citizens, but they cannot block or inhibit trade that crosses state boundaries. Obviously, states have incentives to do so: they may want to favor their own businesses to the disadvantage of companies from other states. But they cannot do that under the DCC.

This doctrine is not exactly clear in the text of the Constitution. It is an extension of the literal Commerce Clause by inference, and not everyone agrees that it is what the Constitution means. But a history of Supreme Court rulings has defined it in a specific way: states may not *discriminate against interstate commerce* or *unduly burden interstate commerce.*[7] In this reading of the document, the negative command of the Commerce Clause was a large part of the point (Congress has the positive authority to regulate interstate trade, while individual states are commanded to not interfere in this realm). However, specific applications of the rule that states can regulate commerce *within* their borders, but not *outside* their borders, run into practical problems. Undue burden standards are notoriously subjective, mostly because they rely on

---

[6]Ibid., page 1, referring to the U.S. Constitution, Article I, Section 8: "The Congress Shall Have Power... To Regulate Commerce with Foreign Nations, and Among the Several States, and with the Indian Tribes."

[7]"First, state regulations may not discriminate against interstate commerce; and second, States may not impose undue burdens on interstate commerce"; "The Court has consistently explained that the Commerce Clause was designed to prevent States from engaging in economic discrimination so they would not divide into isolated, separable units" (*Wayfair* decision, pages 7, 12).

facts rather than on principles: *to what degree is a state law burdening commerce in the real world of facts?*

One way to understand the DCC is that in-state and out-of-state companies are meant to be on the same playing field, without advantage to one side. In this view, the DCC meant to curtail advantages and market distortions. The majority sees the current rule as somewhat perverse in this sense, because it "puts both local businesses and many interstate businesses with physical presence at a competitive disadvantage to remote sellers" (because in-state companies pay sales tax, while out-of-state internet firms do not).[8] The majority points out that Wayfair went so far as to advertise that its customers did not have to pay sales tax; hence the current rule "has come to serve as a judicially created tax shelter" and "rejecting the physical presence rule is necessary to ensure that artificial competitive advantages are not created by this Court's precedent."[9] As Justice Gorsuch phrases it in his concurrence, this is "a judicially created tax break for out-of-state Internet and mail-order firms at the expense of in-state brick-and-mortar rivals."[10]

However, the DCC may not be real. If the Commerce Clause *limits* the states as well as *empowers* the Congress, the Constitution could have said so explicitly, but it does not. According to Justice Thomas, "the negative Commerce Clause has no basis in the Constitution and has proved unworkable in practice."[11] Chief Justice Roberts in his dissent argues that these decisions should be left to Congress and not seized by the Court. But until the Congress acts (if it ever does), does that mean South Dakota *can* do it or that South Dakota *cannot* do it?

---

[8] *Wayfair* decision, page 12.

[9] Ibid., page 13.

[10] *Wayfair* Gorsuch dissent, page 1.

[11] *United Haulers Inc. v. Oneida-Herkimer Solid Waste Management Authority*, 550 U.S. 330 (2007). In Thomas' view, the DCC suggests "the erroneous assumption that the Court must choose between economic protectionism and the free market. But the Constitution vests that fundamentally legislative choice in Congress. To the extent that Congress does not exercise its authority to make that choice, the Constitution does not limit the States' power to regulate commerce. In the face of congressional silence, the States are free to set the balance between protectionism and the free market. Instead of accepting this constitutional reality, the Court's negative Commerce Clause jurisprudence gives nine Justices of this Court the power to decide the appropriate balance." *United Haulers* Thomas dissent, pages 4–5.

What is the default ruling until the Congress decides? The default may be to let states do what they want (and Congress will supersede those laws and settle a national rule if it feels the need); or the default may be to uphold the rule that is most open to free trade; or as Chief Justice Roberts argues, the precedents dictate a default: leave things as they have been.

Precedent and Reliance Interests

In the view of the dissenters, this is not the first time the Court has addressed this issue. Two precedents over the last fifty years have offered a standard. According to *Bellas Hess* in 1967, a mail-order company "whose only connection with customers in the State is by common carrier or the U.S. mail" lacked a minimum requirement of a connection to the state (a "nexus") to allow for taxation. That decision was decided 6 to 3. Twenty-five years later in 1992, the Court reaffirmed the physical presence rule in *Quill* (this time against *North* Dakota).[12] But again, there was dissent; according to Justice Byron White, "there is no relationship between the physical presence/nexus rule the Court retains and Commerce Clause considerations that allegedly justify it."[13] Should the current Court simply follow the precedent that states cannot tax the transactions of companies outside their borders?

One aspect of this question is *reliance interests*, or the expectations that citizens hold and the plans they have made based on the Court's prior rulings. Even the majority concedes that "reliance interests are a legitimate consideration when the Court weighs adherence to an earlier but flawed precedent."[14] The dissenters emphasize "the potential to disrupt the development of such a critical segment of the economy."[15] If a company has to master the tax laws of every state, this may create a

---

[12]*National Bellas Hess, Inc. v. Department of Revenue of Illinois*, 386 U.S. 753 (1967) and *Quill Corp. v. North Dakota*, 504 U.S. 298 (1992).

[13]*Quill* at 327, quoted in *Wayfair* page 9.

[14]*Wayfair* decision, page 20.

[15]*Wayfair* Roberts dissent, page 1.

substantial burden on trade. On the other hand, the majority suggests that software will soon be available to make this simple for companies to do. And no small mom and pop Internet stores need to worry: The South Dakota law only applies to sellers who make at least 200 transactions in the state or ship more than $100,000 worth of goods annually.

Another part of the argument for maintaining *Quill* from twenty-six years ago, and *Bellas Hess* from twenty-five years before that, is respect for *stare decisis* ("to stand by what has been decided"). No legal system can function by revisiting every issue every time, and no legal system can be locked to past conditions and historical errors that may demand correction. *Planned Parenthood v. Casey* (1992) is often considered to be the precedent on precedent. It discussed at length the standards for overruling a past decision or following *stare decisis*, laying out several tests for the legitimate overruling of precedent:

> whether the rule has proven to be intolerable simply in defying *practical workability*; whether the rule is subject to a kind of *reliance* that would lend a special hardship to the consequences of overruling…; whether related *principles of law* have so far developed as to have left the old rule no more than a remnant of abandoned doctrine; or whether *facts have so changed*, or come to be seen so differently, as to have robbed the old rule of significant application or justification.[16] (italics added)

Of the four standards identified in *Casey* (workability, reliance, errors in constitutional principles, and changes in prevailing facts), the *Wayfair* decision depends on the last one: have the facts changed? The majority decision is quite clear that South Dakota is "asking this Court to review these earlier decisions in light of current economic realties."[17] The prior decisions dealt with taxation, but not the new realities of the Internet. This case is not about mail-order, as the precedents are. It is about an entirely different kind of commerce. If e-commerce is not at all comparable to mail-order, then the facts have changed, and the precedents may have to be abandoned.

---

[16]*Casey* decision, 505 U.S. at 854.

[17]*Wayfair* decision, page 4.

Social Facts

Along with constitutional principles that are disputed on the basis of the text and history of the document, the Court also has to define social facts that reflect divided perceptions of reality.[18] How the Supreme Court handles questions of disputed social facts—for example, the influence of racism (as in *Shelby County* in 2013)[19] or the nature of gender differences (as in *Wal-Mart v. Dukes* in 2011)— reflects an underlying debate about our constitutional democracy: who should determine influential social facts when they have come into dispute in our society?

Sometimes the Court cites expert judgment as the basis for a social fact, while at other times, the Court defers to the judgment of one of our representative institutions, like Congress, or a state legislature, or the executive branch.[20] But most of the time, the Justices rely on their own judgment of social facts and provide little justification. In the past, the Court as well as Court-watchers seemed to have assumed that facts were more clear, while principles were hard. This may have reversed: principles are well developed and justified (even if disputed), while

[18]"A social fact is not a statement of principled standard, but an assertion of empirical reality. The core distinction is that principles are normative statements of *what should be*, while facts are empirical statements about *what is*. Statements of fact can be falsified (demonstrated to be incorrect) by empirical evidence (that either exists now or may exist in the future), while statements of principle cannot be falsified regardless of old or new evidence, as they are grounded in judgments of better or worse rather than true or false" (Morgan Marietta and Tyler Farley, "Supreme Facts: The Prevalence and Justification of Social Facts in Landmark Decisions of the Supreme Court," 4, 2 *Journal of Law & Courts* 243–265 (2016), page 244).

[19]In regard to the social facts of racism, see *Schuette v. Coalition to Defend Affirmative Action* (2014) and *Shelby County v. Holder* (2013). One of the facts disputed by the parties in *Shelby County* was the contemporary influence of racism in the Southern states subject to restrictions under the 1965 Voting Rights Act, especially the role of racism in discouraging political participation by minorities (see Chapter 4). Chief Justice John Roberts was the topic of a PolitiFact report on the veracity of his comments on minority political participation (see "Was Chief Justice John Roberts Right About Voting Rates in Massachusetts, Mississippi," 5 March 2013).

[20]See Marietta and Farley "Supreme Facts"; David Faigman, *Constitutional Fictions: A Unified Theory of Constitutional Facts* (New York: Oxford University Press, 2008); Ronald Kahn, *Constructing Individual Rights in a Conservative Age: The Supreme Court and Social Change in the Rehnquist and Roberts Court Eras* (Topeka: University Press of Kansas, 2019); Allison Orr Larsen, "Constitutional Law in an Age of Alternative Facts" 93 *New York Law Review* 175; and Morgan Marietta, *A Citizen's Guide to the Constitution and the Supreme Court* (New York: Routledge, 2014) Chapter 8.

perceptions of facts have fractured and the justifications for upholding one factual perception or another are deeply uncertain.[21]

In deciding such questions, does Congress have the better means of researching and perceiving social facts, or should the Court fill this function? Chief Justice Roberts in dissent emphasizes the role of Congress in determining facts: "As we have said in other DCC cases, Congress has the capacity to investigate and analyze facts beyond anything the Judiciary could match."[22] For this reason and for the preservation of precedent, he "would let Congress decide whether to depart from the physical-presence rule that has governed this area for half a century."[23]

The majority of Justices, however, saw the changes in social facts as compelling regardless of congressional approval. The decision quotes approvingly of several scholars who perceive very different facts between 1992 and 2018, including Walter Hellerstein in the *Harvard Journal of Law & Technology*, who argued in 2000 that we need "rules that are appropriate to the twenty-first century, not the nineteenth."[24] The Court concludes that "each year, the physical presence rule becomes further removed from economic reality."[25] *Wayfair* recognizes that the contemporary economy and Internet have changed, creating a company's presence in a state even when there is no *physical* presence: "a business may be present in a State in a meaningful way without that presence being physical in the traditional sense of the term. A virtual showroom can show far more inventory, in far more detail, and with greater opportunities for consumer and seller interaction than might be possible

---

[21]As Larsen phrases it, we increasingly have "a constitutional law rich in factual claims coupled with an environment where information is very easy to manipulate" (2018, page 179). See Morgan Marietta and David Barker, *One Nation, Two Realities: Dueling Facts in American Democracy* (Oxford University Press, 2019).

[22]*Wayfair* Roberts dissent, page 7.

[23]Ibid.

[24]Walter Hellerstein, "Deconstructing the Debate Over State Taxation of Electronic Commerce," 13 *Harvard Journal of Law & Technology* 549 (2000), cited in *Wayfair* decision, page 9.

[25]*Wayfair* decision, page 10. "Modern e-commerce does not align analytically with a test that relies on the sort of physical presence defined in *Quill*," such that "when the day-to-day functions of marketing and distribution in the modern economy are considered, it is all the more evident that the physical presence rule is artificial in its entirety" (page 14).

for local stores… This Court should not maintain a rule that ignores these substantial virtual connections to the State."[26] In this sense, "the Internet's prevalence and power have changed the dynamics of the national economy."[27] With this in mind, the Court then corrected the previous "false constitutional premise," because "when it decided *Quill* [in 1992], the Court could not have envisioned a world in which the world's largest retailer would be a remote seller [Amazon]."[28] The social facts of the Internet—and hence of commerce—had clearly changed.

Conclusion

Wayfair is about the meaning of the Commerce Clause, but it is more about the meaning of changing social facts and how we recognize them. Some citizens perceive new facts and want the Court to endorse them; they see past precedent as less important than current reality. Others want to leave decisions about prevailing facts to the representative process and defer to Congress, leaving prior rulings in place until democracy takes its course. These approaches to perceptions of facts cut across the common divide between advocates of a living or an original Constitution, and hence *Wayfair* is an unusual kind of 5-4 decision. It may be fitting for *Wayfair* to be Kennedy's last majority opinion, emphasizing his willingness to place evolving social facts at the core of constitutional interpretation.

---

[26]Ibid., page 15.
[27]Ibid., page 18.
[28]Ibid.

9

Justice Neil Gorsuch Joins the Court

Carol Nackenoff and Gilbert Orbea

When Neil Gorsuch was sworn in as Associate Justice of the Supreme Court at the age of 49 on April 10, 2017, his seat had been vacant for 422 days following the death of Justice Antonin Scalia in February 2016. President Obama nominated Merrick Garland, Chief Judge on the U.S. Court of Appeals for the D.C. Circuit to the Court a month later, but the Republican-controlled Senate refused to hold hearings for Judge Garland in a presidential election year. President Trump nominated Judge Gorsuch eleven days after taking office.

Gorsuch's name appeared on the list of judges that Donald Trump released during his 2016 campaign. While releasing such a list was an unusual tactic, campaign lawyer Don McGahn thought it would be

C. Nackenoff (✉)
Political Science, Swarthmore College, Swarthmore, PA, USA

G. Orbea
Political Science and Economics, Swarthmore College,
Swarthmore, PA, USA

© The Author(s) 2019
D. Klein and M. Marietta (eds.), *SCOTUS 2018*,
https://doi.org/10.1007/978-3-030-11255-4_9

a good way to reassure conservatives about Trump's agenda.[1] When publicizing the list of 21 individuals in September 2016 and pledging to choose Supreme Court nominees from this list, Trump singled out the Federalist Society and the Heritage Foundation for their help composing it.[2] Federalist Society executive vice-president Leonard Leo played a major role in assembling the list.[3] Trump told Leo he wanted judges "respected by all, not weak," who would "interpret the Constitution the way the Framers meant it to be."[4] Since the early 1980s, the Federalist Society had been working to groom future members of the judiciary (and other federal officials) who would be reliably conservative and adhere to textualist or originalist readings of the Constitution.[5] According to one scholar, it was "part of an attempt to build an alternative legal elite; one capable of moving conservative and libertarian ideas into the mainstream … [by] training, credentialing, and socializing right-of-center lawyers through its conferences, events and educational programming."[6] Gorsuch has maintained ties with the Federalist network, having spoken at some of their gatherings.

During the confirmation hearings, Gorsuch invoked the "Ginsburg Rule" (attributed to Justice Ruth Bader Ginsburg from her confirmation hearings, admonishing Supreme Court nominees not to signal

---

[1] Joel Achenbach, "How Trump and Two Lawyers Narrowed the Field for His Supreme Court Choice," *The Washington Post*, 8 July 2018.

[2] "Donald J. Trump Finalizes List of Supreme Court Picks" (www.donaldtrumppolicies.com). The first list contained 11 names; five additional names would be added in 2017. The Heritage Foundation claimed credit for five of the names on the first list (Heritage Foundation, "Heritage Expert Helps Shape Supreme Court Nominee List," 14 September 2016).

[3] Achenbach, "How Trump and Two Lawyers Narrowed the Field for His Supreme Court Choice."

[4] Quoted in Jeffrey Toobin, "The Conservative Pipeline to the Supreme Court," *The New Yorker*, 17 April 2017.

[5] Textualism is an approach to interpreting the Constitution that relies on its text and structure above other considerations. In this sense, the document is meant to be read and understood as a complete guide, which can only be altered through amendment; ambiguities in the text should be resolved whenever possible by legislatures rather than courts. This approach can be distinguished from originalism, which relies on greater knowledge of the Founding era and deference to the principles that the Framers meant to convey (often referred to as the "original public meaning" of the Constitution rather than the "intent of the Framers"). See Morgan Marietta, *A Citizen's Guide to the Constitution and the Supreme Court* (New York: Routledge, 2014).

[6] Amanda Hollis-Brusky, Interview with Henry Farrell, Monkey Cage, *The Washington Post*, 17 May 2017.

their views on particular cases or on issues that might come before the Court).[7] Throughout his testimony, he did not reveal his views on cases nor speak about the "correctness" of past precedent. To the frustration of Democratic Senators, Gorsuch did not affirm the correctness of *Brown v. Board of Education*, or other precedents, as concretely as Chief Justice John Roberts had done in his testimony. The hearings also highlighted Judge Gorsuch's anti-regulatory and anti-administrative law stances, evident in past opinions on the 10th Circuit.[8] When questioned repeatedly about the *Chevron* rule (see below), Judge Gorsuch spoke only about how, in a particular 10th Circuit case, he thought its application reached an incorrect result.[9]

Senate Democrats led by Minority Leader Chuck Schumer announced a filibuster of Judge Gorsuch's nomination; among their concerns were the judge's record on workers' rights and the denial of a hearing to Merrick Garland.[10] This announcement led Senate Republicans to invoke the so-called "nuclear option," changing Senate rules to eliminate the filibuster for Supreme Court appointments.[11] The threshold for those nominations would be reduced to a simple majority of senators. Senate Majority Leader Mitch McConnell led the Senate in implementing the new rules, and Gorsuch was confirmed on April 7th, 2017 by a vote of 54–45, with three Democrats joining the Republicans.[12]

---

[7]Lori A. Ringhand and Paul M. Collins Jr., "Neil Gorsuch and the Ginsburg Rules," 93 *Chicago-Kent Law Review* 475 (2018), at 476.

[8]Gillian E. Metzger, "The Supreme Court 2016 Term, Foreword, 1930s Redux: The Administrative State Under Siege," 131 *Harvard Law Review* 1 (2016), fn. 13.

[9]*Gutierrez-Brizuela v. Lynch*, 834 F.3d 1142 (10th Cir. 2016).

[10]Matt Flegenheimer, Charlie Savage, and Adam Liptak, "Democrats Plan to Filibuster to Thwart Gorsuch Nomination," *The New York Times*, 23 March 2017.

[11]See Adam Liptak and Matt Flegenheimer, "Neil Gorsuch Confirmed by Senate as Supreme Court Justice," *The New York Times*, 7 April 2017. The term "nuclear option" was used as a threat by Senate Majority Leader Bill Frist over confirmation battles during George W. Bush's presidency. During President Obama's administration, Democrats led by Majority Leader Harry Reid, frustrated with Republican success at blocking a number of President Obama's nominees, changed the rules to eliminate the filibuster for Cabinet appointees and lower federal court nominees in 2013.

[12]Liptak and Flegenheimer, "Neil Gorsuch Confirmed." The three Democrats in support were Joe Donnelly (IN), Heidi Heitkamp (ND), and Joe Manchin (WV). Heitkamp and Donnelly nevertheless lost their 2018 re-election bids.

Background and Education

Neil McGill Gorsuch was born on August 29, 1967 in Denver, Colorado. He attended a small Catholic elementary and middle school (Christ the King) and Georgetown Preparatory School (Georgetown Prep) in Washington, DC, a prestigious Jesuit boarding school (and the same high school attended by Brett Kavanaugh).[13] He was raised Catholic but now attends an Episcopal church.[14] He attended Columbia University, where he graduated with honors in 1988, and received his J.D. with honors from Harvard Law School in 1991. In 2004, he received a Doctorate of Philosophy from Oxford University. His dissertation on the legality of assisted suicide posited an "incommensurable good" theory which recognizes human life as a "fundamental good," thereby creating a legal prohibition on assisted suicide and euthanasia.[15] Gorsuch clerked for Judge David Sentelle of the Court of Appeals for the D.C. Circuit and Supreme Court Justices Byron White and Anthony Kennedy. In 2006, President George W. Bush nominated Gorsuch to serve on the 10th Circuit based in Denver; he was confirmed unanimously by voice vote.

On the 10th Circuit

While serving on the 10th Circuit Court of Appeals, Judge Gorsuch wrote opinions on a range of issues, many concerning religious liberty. In *Yellowbear v. Lampert*, Gorsuch found a violation of an individual's free exercise of religion under the Religious Land Use and

---

[13]When his mother, Anne M. Gorsuch, was appointed the Administrator of the Environmental Protection Agency (EPA) under President Ronald Reagan in 1981, the family moved to Washington, D.C. She resigned in 1983 and subsequently returned to Colorado to work in private legal practice.

[14]See Mark Matthis and John Frank, "What Neil Gorsuch's Faith and Writings Could Say About His Approach to Religion on the Supreme Court," *Denver Post*, 10 February 2017.

[15]Neil Gorsuch, "The Right to Receive Assistance in Suicide and Euthanasia, with Particular Reference to the Law of the United States," Ph.D. thesis, University of Oxford, 2004, at 357–358. This work was later published as *The Future of Assisted Suicide and Euthanasia* (Princeton: Princeton University Press, 2016), in which he argues that "all human beings are intrinsically valuable and the intentional taking of human life by private persons is always wrong" (page 4).

Institutionalized Persons Act (RLUIPA).[16] Gorsuch also concurred in *Hobby Lobby Stores, Inc. v. Sebelius*, agreeing that the Affordable Care Act's contraceptive mandate substantially burdened religious exercise as guaranteed by the Religious Freedom Restoration Act (RFRA).[17]

Gorsuch echoed Justice Scalia's concern for criminal defendants' rights in several cases, including *United States v. Games-Perez*, insisting "there can be few graver injustices in a society governed by the rule of law than imprisoning a man without requiring proof of his guilt under the written laws of the land."[18] Likewise, in *United States v. Carloss*, a Fourth Amendment challenge to police searching a house covered in "No Trespassing" signs without a warrant, Gorsuch wrote in dissent that such conduct of law enforcement can "claim no basis in our constitutional tradition," a nod both to his judicial philosophy of originalism and textualism as well as a heightened concern for private property rights.[19]

Judicial Philosophy and Evidence of Ideological Location

Various attempts have been made to locate Gorsuch on an ideological spectrum.[20] After the 2016 election, Lee Epstein, Andrew D. Martin and Kevin Quinn predicted then-Judge Gorsuch to be a reliably conservative vote, similar to Justices Scalia and Alito.[21] Another study located Gorsuch as one of the most likely potential nominees to be a consistent voice for originalism on the Court.[22]

---

[16] *Yellowbear v. Lampert*, 741 F.3d 48 (10th Cir. 2014).

[17] *Hobby Lobby Stores, Inc. v. Sebelius*, 723 F.3d 1114 (10th Cir. 2013).

[18] *United States v. Games-Perez*, 695 F.3d 1104, 1117 (10th Cir. 2012).

[19] *United States v. Carloss*, 818 F.3d 988 (10th Cir. 2016).

[20] Alicia Parlapiano and Karen Yourish, "Where Neil Gorsuch Would Fit on the Supreme Court," *The New York Times*, 1 February 2017.

[21] Lee Epstein, Andrew D. Martin, and Kevin Quinn, "President-Elect Trump and His Possible Justices," 15 December 2016, posted at http://epstein.wustl.edu/research/PossibleTrumpJustices.pdf.

[22] Jeremy Kidd, Riddhi Sohan Dasgupta, Ryan Walters, and James Phillips, "Searching for Justice Scalia: Measuring the "Scalia-ness" of the Next Potential Member of the U.S. Supreme Court," 27 January 2017, Available at SSRN.

Gorsuch's judicial philosophy makes him a fitting heir of Antonin Scalia's seat. In a 2016 lecture, Gorsuch paid homage to the late Justice Scalia's textualist approach to constitutional interpretation.[23] Like Scalia, Gorsuch embraced "looking to text, structure, and history to decide what a reasonable reader at the time of the events in question would have understood the law to be."[24] Scalia, he said, understood the difference between judges and legislators—a distinction essential to the preservation of liberty.[25]

Elaborating on textualism during his confirmation hearings, Gorsuch explained the difference between what may have been in the minds of the framers and what they wrote:

> when it comes to equal protection of the laws … it matters not a whit that some of the drafters of the Fourteenth Amendment were racists, because they were, or sexist, because they were. The law they drafted promises equal protection of the laws to all persons. That is what they wrote.[26]

On the bench, Justice Gorsuch has so far been reliably conservative. Andrew Martin and Kevin Quinn have devised a score commonly used to locate Justices on a conservative–liberal ideological spectrum. (Scores above 0 denote conservative, and scores below 0 denote liberal voting patterns.)[27] Justice Gorsuch's score for the October 2017 term was 1.22, making him the third-most conservative Justice, behind Alito (2.18) and Thomas (3.11).[28] Gorsuch scored far more conservatively than Chief Justice Roberts (0.43) and was close to the late Justice Scalia's

---

[23]Neil M. Gorsuch, "Sumner Canary Memorial Lecture: Of Lions and Bears, Judges and Legislators, and the Legacy of Justice Scalia," 66 *Case Western Reserve Law Review* 905–920 (2016).

[24]Ibid., pages 906, 910.

[25]Ibid., pages 910–911, 913.

[26]Senate Hearing 115–208. Reply to Senator Feinstein.

[27]Andrew D. Martin and Kevin M. Quinn, "Dynamic Ideal Point Estimation via Markov Chain Monte Carlo for the U.S. Supreme Court, 1953–1999," 10 *Political Analysis* 134–153 (2002).

[28]Martin-Quinn score measures for the October 2017 term.

average over the last three terms for which he heard arguments (1.57). Using a different measure, Justice Gorsuch voted with Justice Clarence Thomas—considered the Court's most conservative member—84% of the time and with Justice Alito 83% of the time.[29]

Chevron Deference

Whether the Court should defer to rulemaking by federal agencies has become an important topic in the last few years. This issue, usually referred to as *Chevron* deference, is one on which Justice Gorsuch appears to disagree with the late Justice Scalia.[30] The 1984 *Chevron* dispute centered on 1977 amendments to the Clean Air Act. Under Reagan appointee Anne M. Gorsuch (the Justice's mother), the EPA chose to interpret statutory language about a "stationary source" of pollution to permit "bubbling"; this meant a specific source could exceed national air quality standards so long as the plant as a whole did not. The Supreme Court upheld the EPA's relaxed standard: "the fact that the agency has from time to time changed its interpretation of the term 'source' does not… lead us to conclude that no deference should be accorded the agency's interpretation of the statute."[31] The *Chevron* rule has come to mean that where statutory meaning is unclear and does not preclude an administrative agency's interpretation, courts should defer to reasonable rules and definitions of terms formulated by an agency rather than the Court employing its own judgment.

---

[29]Oliver Roeder, "Which Justices Were BFFs This Supreme Court Term," *FiveThirtyEight*, 27 June 2018; See also Adam Feldman, "How Gorsuch's First Year Compares," EmpiricalSCOTUS. com, 11 April 2018.

[30]Antonin Scalia, "Judicial Deference to Administrative Interpretations of Law," 38 *Duke Law Journal* 511–521 (1989) at 515.

[31]*Chevron U.S.A. v. Natural Resources Defense Council* 467 U.S. 837 (1984) at 863–864. If "Congress has not directly addressed the precise question at issue, the Court does not simply impose its own construction of the statute… Rather, if the statute is silent or ambiguous with respect to the specific issue, the question for the Court is whether the agency's answer is based on a permissible construction" (842–843).

Chevron deference has sometimes been viewed as a doctrine of judicial restraint, but it has become increasingly controversial.[32] Critics claim that it is an abdication of judicial responsibility, pointing to problems such as giving agencies free-rein to define the terminology in laws passed by legislatures.[33] In a concurrence in *Gutierrez-Brizuela v. Lynch* when Gorsuch was on the 10th Circuit, he deplored erratic, abrupt, and unjustified policy shifts by administrative agencies and the prospect of agencies "exploiting ambiguous laws... for their own prerogative."[34] Then-judge Gorsuch said, "*Chevron* seems no less than a judge-made doctrine for the abdication of the judicial duty."[35] Justice Scalia had generally embraced *Chevron*.

On the Supreme Court

Justice Gorsuch wasted no time in becoming an active member of the Court; in his first year, he spoke more in oral arguments and wrote more concurring and dissenting opinions than either Justice Sotomayor or Justice Kagan in their first terms.[36] His writing is lively and engaging. Some commentators have been critical of his behavior. Linda Greenhouse, former longtime *New York Times* Court correspondent, described Gorsuch's conduct during his first term as norm-violating and flamboyant, lecturing his colleagues and using a "snarky tone oozing disrespect."[37] Jeffrey Toobin of *The New Yorker* questions Gorsuch's frequent speaking engagements before conservative groups, including

---

[32]Federalist Society, "Why Scalia Was Wrong About Chevron," 23 March 2017 (Suzanna Sherry, Stephen B. Burbank, and Evan Bernick).

[33]See Brett Kavanaugh, "Fixing Statutory Interpretation," 129 *Harvard Law Review* 2118–2163 (2016).

[34]*Gutierrez-Brizuela v. Lynch*, 834 F. 3d 1142 (10th Circuit 2016); see William W. Buzbee, "The Tethered President: Consistency and Contingency in Administrative Law," 98 *Boston University Law Review* 1358–1442.

[35]Gorsuch concurring in *Gutierrez-Brizuela v. Lynch* at 1152.

[36]Stephen Wermiel, "SCOTUS for Law Students: Gorsuch's Start," *SCOTUSBlog*, 29 December 2017.

[37]Linda Greenhouse, "Trump's Life-Tenured Judicial Avatar," *The New York Times*, 6 July 2017.

a speech at the Trump International Hotel, which is currently at the center of Emoluments Clause challenges that the Court may be asked to hear.[38]

Once on the Court, Justice Gorsuch provided a reliable conservative vote through his first term. His vote made the difference in producing a majority opinion in several major cases, usually voting alongside Justices Kennedy, Roberts, Alito, and Thomas. In *Janus v. AFSCME* (see Chapter 4), this majority held that public sector unions could no longer take fees from nonconsenting employees because the practice violates the First Amendment.[39] In another labor relations case delivering a major victory for employers, *Epic Systems Corporation v. Lewis*, Justice Gorsuch wrote for the same majority that agreements requiring individual arbitration must be enforced under the Federal Arbitration Act, language in the National Labor Relations Act notwithstanding.[40]

In *Trump v. Hawaii*, Justice Gorsuch joined the same four Justices to hold that the President's ban on entry to the United States of persons from eight nations was owed deference by the Court; there was no anti-Muslim animus, there were ample national security justifications offered, and the authority of the presidency to regulate the admission of foreign nationals was a fundamental attribute of sovereignty, properly exercised by the political branches (see Chapter 7).[41] In *National Institute of Family and Life Advocates v. Becerra*, Justice Gorsuch joined the same Justices in holding that a California state law requiring pro-life crisis pregnancy centers to notify women about the availability of free or low-cost abortions reflected content-based regulations on speech, violating

---

[38]Jeffrey Toobin, "How Badly Is Neil Gorsuch Annoying the Other Supreme Court Justices?" *The New Yorker*, 29 September 2017. The Emoluments Clause is in Article I: "no Person holding any Office of Profit or Trust under them, shall, without the Consent of Congress, accept any present, Emolument, Office, or Title, of any kind whatever, from any King, Prince, or foreign State." See David Fahrenthold and Jonathan O'Connell, "What Is the Emoluments Clause? Does It Apply to President Trump?" *The Washington Post*, 23 January 2017.

[39]*Janus v. AFSCME*, 585 U.S. ___ (2018).

[40]*Epic Systems Corp. v. Lewis*, 585 U.S. ___ (2018).

[41]*Trump v. Hawaii*, 585 U.S. ___ (2018).

the First Amendment.[42] In *Husted v. A. Philip Randolph Institute*, the same 5-4 majority held that the process used by the State of Ohio to remove persons from its voter lists on change of residence grounds did not violate the National Voter Registration Act (see Chapter 4).[43]

Gorsuch joined a 5-4 decision allowing states to require out-of-state sellers to collect state sales tax (see Chapter 8),[44] a 5-3 decision holding that detained aliens do not have a right to periodic bond hearings,[45] and concurred in a 5-4 decision holding that the Alien Tort Statute (part of the Judiciary Act of 1789) does not permit lawsuits in U.S. courts against foreign corporations by foreigners.[46] He gave more hints of his objections to *Chevron* deference in a written statement (joined by Chief Justice Roberts and Justice Alito) when the Court declined to hear *Scenic America v. Department of Transportation*.[47] Gorsuch dissented in a Fourth Amendment data privacy case, reasoning that when third parties hold someone's electronic data, the Court's reliance on a "reasonable expectations of privacy" standard involved too much judicial intuition about societal norms; he advocated relying instead on definitions of property found in legislation (see Chapter 5).[48] Gorsuch voted with larger majorities on other major cases, including *Murphy v. National Collegiate Athletics Association* (7-2), holding that a federal prohibition on state-authorized sports gambling violated the 10th Amendment's anti-commandeering doctrine supporting state sovereignty.[49] He also joined the 7-2 decision in *Masterpiece Cakeshop*, holding that Colorado's

---

[42]*NIFLA v. Becerra*, 585 U.S. ___ (2018). The Court reversed and remanded, holding that the pro-life pregnancy centers were likely to prevail on the merits.

[43]*Husted v. A. Philip Randolph Institute*, 585 U.S. ___ (2018).

[44]*South Dakota v. Wayfair*, 585 U.S. ___ (2018).

[45]*Jennings v. Rodriguez*, 585 U.S. ___ (2018). Gorsuch did not join Part II.

[46]*Jesner v. Arab Bank*, 585 U.S. ___ (2018). Gorsuch concurred in part and concurred in the judgment.

[47]*Scenic America, Inc. v. Department of Transportation* et al., 583 U.S. ___ (2017).

[48]*Carpenter v. United States*, 585 U.S. ___ (2018). Gorsuch was sympathetic to the argument that the existence of data on third party servers does not extinguish 4th Amendment rights.

[49]*Murphy v. National Collegiate Athletic Association*, 584 U.S. ___ (2018).

Equal Rights Commission had been hostile to religious convictions in ruling against the owners of a bakery who refused to make a wedding cake for a same-sex couple (see Chapter 6).[50]

Justice Gorsuch parted ways with his conservative colleagues on the void-for-vagueness doctrine in *Sessions v. Dimaya*. He agreed with Justices Kagan, Ginsburg, Breyer, and Sotomayor that a section of the Immigration and Nationality Act allowing deportation of those convicted of a "crime of violence" was unconstitutionally vague.[51] He reasoned that the due process clause barred unpredictability, because "vague laws invite arbitrary power."[52] He explicitly rejected Justice Thomas' insistence that the vagueness doctrine lacked grounding in the original meaning of the Constitution's Due Process Clause, instead embracing Justice Scalia's position in an earlier case.[53]

Conclusion

Overall, President Trump can claim victory in the nomination and seating of Justice Neil Gorsuch. His promise to appoint someone in the vein of Antonin Scalia—from his originalist judicial philosophy, to his stature and intellect, to his engaging writing—was kept. Gorsuch's solidly conservative background on the 10th Circuit has, so far, translated into a reliable vote for the conservative bloc of the Supreme Court. Given his age, Justice Gorsuch will likely be a major force on the Court for the next three to four decades.

---

[50]The Supreme Court has been asked to grant certiorari in the case of *Klein v. Oregon Bureau of Labor and Industries*. The petition affords the Court an opportunity to expand on *Masterpiece Cakeshop* by determining how much religious accommodation must be accorded to state anti-discrimination statutes.

[51]18 U.S.C §16(b). Gorsuch concurred in part and concurred in the judgment.

[52]*Sessions v. Dimaya*, 584 U.S. ___ (2018), Gorsuch concurrence, page 1. Gorsuch insisted (at 18) he was making a very narrow, procedural point and that legislatures were free to pursue the ends they choose.

[53]*Sessions v. Dimaya* Thomas dissent at pages 2–16; Scalia writing for the Court in *Johnson v. United States* (2015).

10

Justice Anthony Kennedy Retires (1988–2018)

Morgan Marietta

The law is the story of our moral life.

Anthony Kennedy, July 26, 2018

Anthony Kennedy wrote both *Obergefell* and *Citizens United*. From the perspective of political liberals, his legacy is half valiant and half dastardly, upholding gay rights while allowing corporate money to corrupt democracy; political conservatives equally see him as half right and half wrong, grounded in the opposite aspects of his legacy. Political science models that explain Justices in simple terms of political ideology simply cannot account for one of the most influential Justices of post-World War II America. Kennedy was a quiet lion of an independent-minded judiciary, whose presence determined many outcomes of a divided Supreme Court and whose departure signals a dramatic shift in the future of the Court.

M. Marietta (✉)
Department of Political Science,
University of Massachusetts Lowell, Lowell, MA, USA

© The Author(s) 2019
D. Klein and M. Marietta (eds.), *SCOTUS 2018*,
https://doi.org/10.1007/978-3-030-11255-4_10

111

Kennedy's Legacies

Kennedy offers dual legacies: often described as a swing voter, but on the whole more conservative than not; defender of both free speech and gay rights, which came into conflict during his last term in *Masterpiece Cakeshop*; loved and hated by many citizens as the Justice who upheld and abandoned their causes in the critical 5-4 cases. Justice Kennedy emerged in the tumultuous conflict over the nomination of arch-conservative Robert Bork, and his departure spurred the public conflict over the nomination of Brett Kavanaugh. Like Kennedy's nomination and retirement, his legacies are a reflection of the divided political and constitutional culture of contemporary politics.

Toward the end of his second term, President Ronald Reagan nominated Robert Bork—an undisputed conservative intellectual and unabashed originalist with a long written record of his thinking combined with a willingness to discuss it. Bork was Reagan's third nomination to the Court, following Sandra Day O'Connor and Antonin Scalia. The contentious fight and ultimate rejection by the Senate began the new era of partisan dispute over Supreme Court nominations; while O'Connor and Scalia were approved without dissent (99/0 and 98/0), Bork was rejected by a vote of 58/42. The replacement selection—the now mostly forgotten other Ginsburg, not Ruth Bader Ginsburg, but Douglas Ginsburg—withdrew from consideration after revelations of pot smoking while a professor at Harvard. The final compromise selection was Anthony Kennedy, whose thirty years to follow as one of the least-predictable Justices on the Court reflected the circumstances of his nomination. He was selected amidst polarized partisan conflict to be confirmed more easily; he served during a polarized time as the somewhat-swing voter; and his retirement sparked renewed partisan conflict over his replacement, who would likely shift the balance of the Court.

While Kennedy was often discussed as a swing-voter, he often swung more right than left. In his last term (summarized in this book), he ruled with the conservatives on all of the major decisions, including *Trump, Janus, Carpenter, Husted,* and *Masterpiece Cakeshop*. In addition to *Citizens United* (2010), he ruled with the conservatives in *Lopez* (1995) limiting the power of Congress under the Commerce Clause (5-4); with the conservatives in *Grutter v. Bollinger* (2003) opposing affirmative action as violating equal protection (on the losing side of the 5-4); with the conservatives in *Heller* (2008) on recognizing gun rights as fundamental under the Second Amendment (5-4); with the conservatives in *NFIB v. Sebelius* (2012) on the constitutionality of Obamacare (again on the losing side of the 5-4); and with the conservatives in *Shelby County* (2013) limiting the Voting Rights Act of 1965 (5-4). However, he is best known for his liberal rulings on free speech and especially gay rights. To try to understand this in terms of allegiance to Left or Right policy outcomes is to misunderstand both Kennedy and the Court. Kennedy was not a political ideologue. Nor was he a "moderate," a term which has little meaning. He had distinct views of the Constitution that were not directly partisan, but represented a different way of seeing the role of a Justice of the Supreme Court, a way that will be missed.

Kennedy's approach to the Constitution can be understood in a few different ways. One is that he did not agree with either the originalists or the living constitutionalists on how the Constitution should be read. The originalists believe the document should be read for the intent of its authors (the 'original public meaning'). That meaning is fixed until amended; hence, the principles of the Constitution do not change (though prevailing social facts do). Living constitutionalists, on the other hand, argue that we should read the document as contemporary Americans do, especially in regard to concepts like liberty and equality, whose meanings have shifted. Principles of the Constitution *can* alter or emerge over time (like privacy or dignity). Prevailing social facts can change as well, which may demand a shift in principles. Another way of phrasing the debate between advocates of an original or a living Constitution is whether the primary responsibility for recognizing change is the duty of *legislatures* or *courts*. Can the Justices recognize expanded rights under new conditions, or is that the province of electoral democracy rather than judicial democracy? One side trusts Justices to perceive changes in constitutional principles, while the other side does not. One side trusts citizens to govern through elections unless the outcome blatantly violates a clear constitutional protection, while the other side does not.

Kennedy was not persuaded by either of these views. He was neither an originalist nor a living constitutionalist, but more of a *common law* constitutionalist.[1] He sought incremental changes responding to new challenges, seeking a workable rule that addresses real-world circumstances rather than a devotion to an abstract school of interpretation. He upheld a *personal* and *pragmatic* as well as principled Constitution. Speaking to the Ninth Circuit Judicial Conference after announcing his retirement, Kennedy said that, "behind the cases there's always a real person. That's the whole idea and meaning of the law." Kennedy's quote in the headnote to this chapter echoes Oliver Wendell Holmes Jr.'s famous line that the life of the law is not logic, but experience.[2] Kennedy was acutely aware of the personal impact of the Court's decisions and the practical concerns of how those decisions are implemented.

Another way to summarize Kennedy's legacy is his deep commitment to a free society. Many Americans think of Kennedy as an advocate of gay rights. He was not. *He was an advocate of a free society, which led to gay rights.* He was also an advocate of other aspects of a free society, such as freedom of speech and freedom of religion. Kennedy did not see these liberties as contradictory, even when advocates of one policy or the other thought they were. The three domains for which Kennedy is best known illustrate his dual legacy of liberty and pragmatism: abortion, free speech, and gay rights. In all of these areas, he tended to join the liberal side of the Court (though not always), but perhaps more importantly, he defined the *type* of liberal decision that was delivered, shaping these areas of constitutional law.

---

[1]For a summary of the competing approaches to reading the Constitution, see Marietta, *A Citizen's Guide to the Constitution and the Supreme Court* (New York: Routledge, 2014).

[2]"The life of the law has not been logic: it has been experience… The law embodies the story of a nation's development through many centuries, and it cannot be dealt with as if it contained only the axioms and corollaries of a book of mathematics." *The Common Law* 1881.

Abortion

When *Roe v. Wade* from 1973 was re-visited in 1992, it looked like the Court might overturn the constitutionally protected right of abortion in the United States. Kennedy co-authored the controlling opinion in *Casey* (with O'Connor and Souter) that upheld the core of *Roe*, while allowing regulations of abortion that did not create an undue burden on the right.[3] However, in 2007, Kennedy sided with the conservatives to uphold the constitutionality of state laws banning late-term abortions. He wrote the decision that allowed such regulations on the grounds of the gruesome facts of the procedure.[4] While some criticized him for dwelling on the descriptions of the medical procedure, Kennedy saw clear facts as important; if "law is the story of our moral life" (as Kennedy said at the end of his career), then the facts of that life matter, they change over time, and they should be witnessed forthrightly.[5] In 2016, he sided with the liberals in *Whole Woman's Health* to strike down the Texas effort to regulate safety provisions in a way that would force the closing of the few clinics in the state.[6] Again, the facts on the ground mattered as much as the principles. And this last term in *NIFLA* (discussed in Chapter 5), he ruled with the conservatives that organizations counseling against abortion were protected from a state regulation forcing them to provide specific information about the availability of abortion services. In each case, the right of privacy that protects the abortion decision was maintained, but the specific facts of the surrounding circumstances counted as well. For the last thirty years, Kennedy's combination of principle and pragmatism defined the law of abortion in the United States: legal but limited.

---

[3] *Planned Parenthood v. Casey*, 505 U.S. 833 (1992).

[4] Kennedy describes the late-term abortion procedure as allowing a doctor to "pierce the skull and vacuum the fast-developing brain" of "an unborn child, a child assuming the human form." *Gonzales v. Carhart* 505 U.S. 124 (2007).

[5] Others criticized Kennedy's mention of the possibility that women would come to regret the abortion decision, one of the perceived facts that Kennedy endorsed but others thought had no foundation.

[6] *Whole Woman's Health v. Hellerstedt*, 579 U.S. ___ (2016).

Free Speech

Right after Kennedy came to the Court, it heard the famous flag burning case of *Texas v. Johnson*. Kennedy joined the majority opinion written by Justice Brennan (5-4), but also wrote a concurrence:

> The hard fact is that sometimes we must make decisions we do not like. We make them because they are right, right in the sense that the law and the Constitution, as we see them, compel the result....
>
> The case here today forces recognition of the costs to which those beliefs commit us. It is poignant but fundamental that the flag protects those who hold it in contempt.[7]

A few years later, Kennedy wrote that "the First Amendment is often inconvenient."[8] It is also often unpopular, which was the case when the Westboro Baptist Church picketed the funeral of a fallen Marine and held signs expressing hateful sentiments. But in *Snyder v. Phelps* in 2011, Kennedy joined Chief Justice Roberts' opinion upholding the right of expression, even in these circumstances. In *Alvarez* in 2012, Kennedy also upheld a constitutionally protected right to lie about military medals awarded, striking down the Stolen Valor Act. To Kennedy—like to Scalia in regard to flag burning—such behavior is repulsive but protected, given the higher principle that "The remedy for speech that is false is speech that is true. This is the ordinary course in a free society. The response to the unreasoned is the rational; to the uninformed, the enlightened; to the straight-out lie, the simple truth."[9]

This principled view of free speech regardless of surrounding circumstances was Kennedy's stance in perhaps his least popular decision, *Citizens United*:

---

[7] *Texas v. Johnson* Kennedy concurrence, 491 U.S. 397 (1989) at 421.
[8] *Krishnas v. Lee* Kennedy concurrence, 505 U.S. 672 (1992) at 701.
[9] *U.S. v. Alvarez*, 567 U.S. 709 (2012).

When Government seeks to use its full power, including the criminal law, to command where a person may get his or her information or what distrusted source he or she may not hear, it uses censorship to control thought. This is unlawful. The First Amendment confirms the freedom to think for ourselves.[10]

Whether it annoys the Left in *Citizens* or the Right in *Alvarez*, Kennedy believed free speech was triumphant. His ruling in *Citizens* protected the free speech rights (and therefore the right to contribute money) of corporations. Kennedy has been criticized in this ruling for not taking into account the surrounding facts of corporate speech and its potential to drown out the representation of living citizen voters.[11] But Kennedy is convinced that freedom of speech is a higher principle and a stronger bulwark of democracy. In the free speech cases this term—*Janus* and *NIFLA* (see Chapter 5)—Kennedy clarified the dangers of coerced speech as "the serious threat presented when government seeks to impose its own message in the place of individual speech, thought, and expression… Government must not be allowed to force persons to express a message contrary to their deepest convictions."[12]

Gay Rights

Kennedy wrote the four major gay rights decisions of the last three decades: *Romer, Lawrence, Windsor,* and *Obergefell*. He also wrote the decision that limited this line of rulings in *Masterpiece Cakeshop*. During a time-period in which public attitudes toward the acceptance and normality of LGBT sexual identity shifted dramatically, Kennedy adapted the law of the Constitution to these changing social facts.

---

[10]*Citizens United v. Federal Election Commission*, 558 U.S. 310 (2010) at 356.

[11]Kennedy also perceived that corporate contributions do not lead to corruption ("this Court now concludes that independent expenditures, including those made by corporations, do not give rise to corruption or the appearance of corruption" *Citizens* at 314), again a perceived fact that is deeply disputed.

[12]*NIFLA v. Becerra* Kennedy concurrence, pages 1 and 2.

The cases begin and end in Colorado. *Romer v. Evans* in 1996 struck down an amendment to the Colorado state constitution (approved by voter initiative), disallowing any state action affording LGBT citizens "to have or claim any minority status, quota preferences, protected status or claim of discrimination." Kennedy wrote that this amendment raised "the inevitable inference" that it was "born of animosity toward the class of persons affected," reflecting a "desire to harm a politically unpopular group."[13] Seven years later in 2003, Kennedy wrote the most far-reaching gay rights decision to that time in *Lawrence v. Texas*, ruling that state laws criminalizing homosexuality were unconstitutional. A state's power to regulate society was limited to health and safety, but did not extend to morality. A decade later, the Court began to address the public controversy over same-sex marriage by first considering the definition of marriage codified in DOMA (the Defense of Marriage Act signed by President Bill Clinton in 1996). *U.S. v. Windsor* in 2013 was a tax case, in which Edith Windsor had been denied the federal estate tax exemption for surviving spouses (which she would have been granted had her spouse been a man).[14] Kennedy ruled that DOMA's definition of marriage treated heterosexual marriages and same-sex marriages differently in a way that violated due process and equal protection. The most important case, however, was *Obergefell v. Hodges* in 2015, which overturned all bans on gay marriage in all states, ruling that same-sex marriages were constitutionally protected. Together, these four rulings established in sequence between 1996 and 2015 that states could not openly target gay citizens; that laws criminalizing homosexuality were unconstitutional; that the federal government lacked the power to define marriage as one man and one woman; and finally that same-sex marriage had to be recognized. Kennedy was the architect of all of these decisions and their constitutional foundations.

---

[13] *Romer v. Evans*, 517 U.S. 620 (1996) at 634.

[14] At this time, same-sex marriage was recognized in New York State, but federal law (DOMA) defined marriage as "only a legal union between one man and one woman as husband and wife."

While the legal results in these cases were celebrated in many quarters, many readers still questioned if Kennedy was building the firmest constitutional basis for the rulings. The culminating decision in *Obergefell* ruled that marriage is a fundamental right and therefore a state limitation on how individuals define that institution is a violation of the Constitution. This is not what many scholars expected the Court to do. Kennedy may have been on stronger ground by expanding the Equal Protection Clause to encompass gay rights, arguing that Equal Protection applies to sexuality as well as to race and gender as a protected class. Alternatively, I believe he would have been on stronger ground to have stated that the Establishment Clause of the First Amendment forbids laws that are essentially religious or clearly religiously motivated, which includes bans on gay marriage. However, Kennedy's approach to gay rights rested on the concept of dignity.[15]

In *Lawrence*:

> adults may choose to enter upon this relationship in the confines of their homes and their own private lives and still retain their dignity as free persons

> The stigma this criminal statute imposes, moreover, is not trivial. The offense, to be sure, is but a class C misdemeanor, a minor offense in the Texas legal system. Still, it remains a criminal offense with all that imports for the dignity of the persons charged.[16]

Speaking of marriage in *Windsor*:

> Responsibilities, as well as rights, enhance the dignity and integrity of the person.

> DOMA undermines both the public and private significance of state-sanctioned same-sex marriages; for it tells those couples, and all the world, that their otherwise valid marriages are unworthy of federal

---

[15]See the discussion of dignity in Chapter 6 on *Masterpiece Cakeshop*.
[16]*Lawrence v. Texas*, 539 U.S. 558 (2003) at 567, 575.

recognition. This places same-sex couples in an unstable position of being in a second-tier marriage. The differentiation demeans the couple... whose relationship the State has sought to dignify.[17]

But especially in *Obergefell*:

The lifelong union of a man and a woman always has promised nobility and dignity to all persons, without regard to their station in life.

There is dignity in the bond between two men or two women who seek to marry and in their autonomy to make such profound choices.

The final sentences of the ruling are, "They ask for equal dignity in the eyes of the law. The Constitution grants them that right."[18] While dignity has a certain rhetorical appeal, it may be more compelling than constitutional (see Chapter 6).[19] Many have argued that dignity is not the strongest reed on which to rest constitutional decisions, given that (1) it is not protected in the text of the Constitution and (2) it applies to many holders of rights whose claims may conflict (including both LGBT citizens and religious observers). In his dissent to *Obergefell*, Justice Thomas provides an entirely different rejoinder to dignity as a foundation for law: "it rejects the idea—captured in our Declaration of Independence—that human dignity is innate and suggests that instead it comes from the government."[20] Thomas's point illustrates the lack of clarity in what dignity as a constitutional concept entails, especially who holds it, or who holds more of it than someone else, or who could take it away.

Kennedy clearly believed that dignity was an aspect of marriage and of the autonomy to identify one's own sexuality, but he also believed that several other claims to rights reflected aspects of dignity. In an Eighth

---

[17] *U.S. v. Windsor*, 570 U.S. 744 (2013), slip opinion page 22.

[18] *Obergefell* decision, pages 3, 13, 28.

[19] Justice Scalia criticized Kennedy's phrasing in *Obergefell* as "mummeries and straining-to-be-memorable passages," comparing his opening sentence to "the mystical aphorisms of the fortune cookie." *Obergefell* Scalia dissent, pages 4, 8.

[20] *Obergefell* Thomas dissent, page 1.

Amendment case on the death penalty, Kennedy invoked "the dignity of all persons."[21] In *Casey* on abortion rights, he described such decisions as "the most intimate and personal choices a person may make in a lifetime, choices central to personal dignity and autonomy."[22] In his ruling for the majority in *Akron Center* in 1990 (upholding the constitutionality of restrictions on minors seeking an abortion), he wrote of the dignity of the woman ("her decision will embrace her own destiny and personal dignity"), but four sentences later of the dignity of the minor's family. ("It would deny all dignity to the family to say that the State cannot take this reasonable step in regulating its health professions to ensure that, in most cases, a young woman will receive guidance and understanding from a parent.")[23] Perhaps most significantly for his decision in *Masterpiece Cakeshop*, Kennedy argued that dignity also applies to religious believers: "In our constitutional tradition, freedom means that all persons have the right to believe or strive to believe in a divine creator and a divine law. For those who choose this course, free exercise is essential in preserving their own dignity and in striving for a self-definition shaped by their religious precepts."[24]

Returning to Colorado in *Masterpiece Cakeshop* in 2018—three years after *Obergefell* and 22 years after *Romer*—Kennedy addressed the competing claims of the dignity of a gay couple seeking a wedding cake and the religious liberty of a baker who did not wish to fashion a cake to celebrate their wedding. In the oral arguments, Kennedy asserted that the treatment of Christians by the state of Colorado was "neither tolerant nor respectful," as the Constitution requires.[25] The couple held dignity, but so did the baker. The line of gay rights decisions grounded in dignity had reached their limit. Kennedy sees dignity as inherent in several aspects of democratic life, all equally protected by the Constitution.

---

[21] *Roper v. Simmons* 543 U.S. 551 (2005) at 560.

[22] *Casey*, 505 U.S. at 851.

[23] *Ohio v. Akron Center for Reproductive Health*, 497 U.S. 502 (1990) at 520.

[24] *Burwell v. Hobby Lobby Stores, Inc.* 573 U.S. ___ (2014), Kennedy concurrence, pages 1–2.

[25] *Masterpiece Cakeshop* oral arguments transcript, 5 December 2017, page 62.

In the end, we are left to evaluate the implications of Kennedy's core argument that dignity is implicit in the Constitution's broader meaning and that it reinforces a range of rights from government interference.

Kennedy's willingness to look beyond the text of the Constitution and promote the higher calling of liberty led to some of his best writings. In *Lawrence v. Texas*:

> Had those who drew and ratified the Due Process Clauses of the Fifth Amendment or the Fourteenth Amendment known the components of liberty in its manifold possibilities, they might have been more specific. They did not presume to have this insight. They knew times can blind us to certain truths and later generations can see that laws once thought necessary and proper in fact serve only to oppress. As the Constitution endures, persons in every generation can invoke its principles in their own search for greater freedom.[26]

Kennedy's greatest legacies—and where he is most open to critique—are in the areas where he led the development of constitutional law in a bold fashion that established new rights at the confluence of expanding liberty and evolving circumstances. His legacy is high-minded, but perhaps ungrounded; path-breaking, but perhaps not on a clear path that future decisions can follow. His approach has its critics and has perhaps reached its limit, but it shaped constitutional law in our era. Many have argued that Kennedy swung left on policy when it came to gay rights, free speech, and abortion; he did not—he swung in favor of *liberty tempered by changing facts*. He was deeply committed to a free society, which was free and dignified for all people, encompassing freedom of speech, freedom of reproductive autonomy, freedom of sexual expression, and freedom of religious expression. He felt the need to examine changing social facts as well as constitutional principles, leading to a complex legacy that defies the more common categories of thought.

---

[26]*Lawrence v. Texas*, 539 U.S. 562 (2003) at 578–579.

The Post-Kennedy Court

Scalia's replacement with Gorsuch did not fundamentally shift the Court, but Kennedy's replacement with Kavanaugh will certainly do so. Kennedy's departure leaves the Court comprised of originalists (Thomas, Gorsuch, and Kavanaugh), quasi-originalists (Alito and Roberts, who hold greater regard for precedent and concern for the political ramifications of the Court's decisions), and living constitutionalists who are aging (as of 2019, Kagan is late 50s, Sotomayor mid 60s, Breyer early 80s, and Ginsburg mid 80s). The future balance of the Court depends on how long President Trump can remain in office versus how long the liberal Justices can remain on the bench. The previous 4-1-4 Court— Breyer, Ginsburg, Kagan, and Sotomayor on the left, Kennedy in the middle, and Alito, Gorsuch, Roberts, and Thomas on the right—has been replaced by a 5-4 conservative Court. If Thomas retires strategically before Trump faces re-election, this would allow a Republican President and Senate to replace him, cementing a longer term conservative majority. If one more liberal Justice is replaced with a judicial conservative during Trump's presidency, this would move the Court to a 6-3 conservative majority, leading to deeper and longer lasting effects. So the Court's composition faces two competing timelines: Trump's longevity in office and the current Justices' longevity on the Court. Who can stay longer, Trump facing investigation and the 2020 election or the Justices facing time?

A conservative or originalist Court has not existed in contemporary (post-World War II) American politics, so its potential influence is not fully appreciated. Such a Court will focus on the specific limits of the written document, emphasizing the bounds, principles, and rights recognized under the original Constitution: boundaries on federal government power; principles such as federalism, ordered liberty, and separation of powers; and the rights that are clear and enumerated. This will lead to rulings that emphasize electoral democracy over judicial democracy, raising the power of state legislatures and lowering the role of the Court in overturning their actions. The shift toward a majority of originalists (or at least conservatives) will likely mean that the recognition of new rights will cease; gun rights will be recognized more fully; the Interstate Commerce Clause will contract, limiting the power of Congress to enact regulation; First Amendment rights to freedom of religious exercise and freedom of speech will be recognized more broadly; separation of powers will be enforced against bureaucracies, meaning that executive branch agencies will be seen as less independent and less empowered to enforce regulations not enacted by Congress; affirmative action will face greater scrutiny and limitation; and the executive branch will be allowed greater deference to act on perceived threats to security. In the three areas of Kennedy's core legacy, abortion rights under the right of privacy will likely contract (though how far is unknown); gay rights have likely reached their limit; and free speech will likely maintain Kennedy's position of a strong First Amendment reflecting both speech and religious exercise.

These suggestions about the future are, of course, speculative. Kennedy saw the law as oriented toward the future, as a promise: "For us law is a promise. It's a promise of liberty, it's a promise of freedom, it's a promise that we can plan our own destiny. And that's what we do as lawyers. That's what we do as judges."[27] He also believed in the teaching role of the Court. Essentially home-schooled as a child by his teacher mother and attorney father, he went on to teach evening courses in law school for twenty years before joining the Supreme Court. He saw the Court's work as a form of persuasion combining principle and practicality: "Over time I think the Supreme Court is a majoritarian institution: the majority of the country begins to see that these litigants, these people, real people, had a real injury the Court addressed, and our commitment to the rule of law, our commitment to decency, is such that most of our decisions are accepted over time."[28] He did not want the Court to teach an ideological vision of a living Constitution or an original Constitution. He seemed to believe in a problem-solving and teaching Constitution, in some degree a personal Constitution that protected individual dignity in ways that conflict as well as intersect. His was a complex Constitution for simpler times, on its way to being replaced by the opposite.

---

[27]Speech to the Ninth Circuit Judicial Conference, 26 July 2018.
[28]Ibid.

11

The Troubled Confirmation of Justice Brett Kavanaugh

Julie Novkov

For several years, Supreme Court nominations have followed a fairly standard practice. A vacancy occurs, the President announces a nominee, initial public discussion occurs, and in almost all cases, the nominee moves forward to the confirmation process. Since Ronald Reagan became President, only one nominee—Robert Bork—has been rejected in a Senate vote. The confirmation process itself has also become a predictable form of political theatre. Members of the Senate Judiciary Committee express their judicial philosophies and support or opposition to lightning-rod precedents, at times interest groups raise funds to support or oppose nominees, and the nominees themselves play their cards close to the vest, expressing fidelity to uncontroversial legal principles and judicial standards. In two instances, however, the script was shattered by unanticipated allegations of sexual misconduct. One was more than a quarter century ago, when Anita Hill accused nominee Clarence Thomas of sexually harassing her when he supervised her at the Equal Employment Opportunity Commission. The second played

J. Novkov (✉)
University at Albany, SUNY, Albany, NY, USA

© The Author(s) 2019
D. Klein and M. Marietta (eds.), *SCOTUS 2018*,
https://doi.org/10.1007/978-3-030-11255-4_11

out in September and early October 2018, as a nation primed by the #MeToo movement's revelations of past sexual misconduct divided bitterly over Christine Blasey Ford and other women's claims that nominee Brett Kavanaugh was a sexual assailant.

On June 26, 2018, Associate Justice Anthony Kennedy, an eighty-one-year old with thirty years' service on the Court, announced that he was stepping down. His decision to resign left President Donald Trump with the potential to transform the institution, and thereby American law, in a more conservative direction for years to come.

On July 9, Donald Trump introduced Brett Kavanaugh as his choice to take Justice Kennedy's vacated seat. Kavanaugh had impeccable conservative credentials, and his nomination was unsurprising to those in the know. He had worked under Kenneth Starr during Starr's service as Independent Counsel in the investigation that led to President Bill Clinton's impeachment, authoring the Starr Report.[1] He also served as an aide to George W. Bush, earning as a reward a seat on the influential D.C. Circuit Court in 2006.[2] His pedigree included a stint as a clerk for 9th Circuit Judge Alex Kozinski (who retired after several former clerks and junior staffers accused him of sexual harassment), and then a clerking position for Justice Kennedy himself.[3] An engaged Catholic, Kavanaugh volunteered for Catholic Charities in Washington, DC, and sat on the board of directors for Washington Jesuit Academy, where he also tutored.[4] His consciously constructed professional trajectory from his years at Yale Law School up to the point when he stood next to Trump as the nominee seemed to present a clear, unbroken narrative that could lead only and triumphantly to the U.S. Supreme Court.

While Kavanaugh was ultimately confirmed, the struggle over his confirmation was one of the most bitter, publicly controversial, and partisan confirmation fights in U.S. history, generating levels of investment

---

[1]Matthew Nussbaum, "Brett Kavanaugh: Who Is He? Bio, Facts, Background, and Political Views," *Politico*, 9 July 2018.

[2]Ibid.

[3]Sophie Tatum, "Kavanaugh Contacted Kozinski After Resignation Because He Was 'Concerned About His Mental Health'," *CNN*, 13 September 2018.

[4]Nussbaum, "Brett Kavanaugh: Who Is He?"

and anger only reached during debates over Robert Bork, who was denied confirmation in 1987, and Clarence Thomas, who was seated on the Court in 1991. Even before allegations of sexual assault against him became public, Kavanaugh was unusually controversial; an August CNN poll found that he had less support for confirmation than thirty years' worth of prior nominees, including failed nominee Harriet Miers; only Bork was initially less popular.[5] The confirmation struggle developed as a play with two acts. The first was the usual investigative stage, featuring strong opposition by Democrats but overshadowed by something of an air of inevitability in light of the Senate's elimination of the filibuster and the Democrats' minority status. The second, as in the case of Clarence Thomas, erupted after sexual misconduct allegations became public in September. The long-term legacy is likely to be the reinforcement of highly partisan mobilization around Supreme Court vacancies. And as with the Thomas nomination, the national conversation over Kavanaugh, while it briefly increased concern about sexual assault and its long-term consequences, does not yet appear to be driving major policy changes or cultural shifts.

Stage One: A Heated but Predetermined Struggle

The nomination of an individual for a seat on the U.S. Supreme Court initiates a process that has been in place since the late 1960s. Once the President announces the nominee, the consideration of the candidate shifts to the Senate Judiciary Committee. The Judiciary Committee's process has three stages: (1) an investigative stage that precedes any formal hearings, (2) public hearings, in which committee members have

---

[5]Jennifer Agiesta, "CNN Poll: Brett Kavanaugh Nomination Has Lowest Public Support Since Robert Bork," *CNN Politics*, 16 August 2018.

the opportunity to question the nominee, and finally (3) a committee vote and preparation of a recommendation on the candidate to the full Senate.[6]

The pre-hearing investigation is comprehensive. The FBI conducts an independent investigation. The American Bar Association reviews the nominee, rating the person as well qualified, qualified, or not qualified.[7] And the nominee completes a lengthy questionnaire, which elicits a detailed professional and personal biography as well as extensive financial information.

The period before the Judiciary Committee's hearings began saw two significant controversies erupt around Kavanaugh's nomination. The first concerned his public writings and statements about investigations of Presidents. The second was about materials not released for full review.

Since Robert Bork's nomination in the 1980s, nominees' prior writings have invited scrutiny. Kavanaugh's writings were no exception, and his opponents quickly found fodder for criticism. Of particular interest was a piece he authored entitled "The President and the Independent Counsel," which reflected on his experience as Kenneth Starr's Associate Counsel during the Whitewater investigation.[8] Kavanaugh recommended that "Congress should establish that the President can be indicted only after he leaves office voluntarily or is impeached by the House of Representatives and convicted and removed by the Senate."[9] Kavanaugh argued that the current system structures the relationship between the President and the independent counsel in too adversarial a fashion, creating disincentives for the kind of cooperation that could solve significant problems.

Arguing from an originalist standpoint, Kavanaugh claimed that Congress, not an independent counsel, has both the right and the duty to manage any investigative process that touches the presidency.[10]

---

[6]Barry McMillion, "Supreme Court Appointment Process: Consideration by the Senate Judiciary Committee," Washington, DC: Congressional Research Service, 14 August 2018.

[7]Ibid.

[8]Brett Kavanaugh, "The President and the Independent Counsel," 86 *Georgetown Law Journal* 2133–2178 (1998).

[9]Ibid., page 2137.

[10]Ibid., page 2158.

He further argued that indicting a sitting President for any crime is constitutionally questionable, because it has the potential to disable both the government on the whole and the indicted President's party.[11] In Kavanaugh's view in 1998, "If Congress declines to investigate, or to impeach and remove the President, there can be no criminal prosecution at least until his term in office expires."[12]

The topic arose again in an article that Kavanaugh published in 2009, while Barack Obama was president. Kavanaugh suggested that Congress pass a statute preventing civil suits, criminal investigations, and criminal prosecutions against the president during his term of office.[13] The article did not argue in favor of complete immunity, but rather for the wisdom of deferring the President's direct involvement in litigation while in office. Kavanaugh did acknowledge that some behavior by a President might be serious enough to warrant immediate action, but argued that such action should be undertaken by Congress, not an independent prosecutor or other actor. (Ironically, in the same article, Kavanaugh argued for a Senate rule requiring consideration and an up-or-down vote on every judicial nominee within 180 days of nomination by a president, a stance completely at odds with the Senate's treatment of Obama nominee Merrick Garland.[14])

Finally, when speaking at a conservative event in 2016, Kavanaugh identified *Morrison v. Olson* as a case that he would like to see overturned. The ruling upheld the Independent Counsel Act, which authorizes the appointment of an independent investigator to explore allegations of governmental misconduct.[15]

Kavanaugh's remarks provoked vigorous reactions from leading Senate Democrats, who criticized him as potentially biased against the ongoing investigation of President Trump by Robert Mueller.[16]

---

[11]Ibid., page 2157.

[12]Ibid., page 2161.

[13]Brett Kavanaugh, "Separation of Powers During the Forty-Fourth Presidency and Beyond," 93 *Minnesota Law Review* 1454–1486 (2009) at 1461.

[14]Ibid., page 1468.

[15]*Morrison v. Olson*, 487 U.S. 654 (1988).

[16]Jane Timm, "Trump Supreme Court Pick Kavanaugh: 'I'd Put the Final Nail' in Independent Counsel Precedent," *NBC News*, 18 July 2018.

Caroline Frederickson, President of the American Constitution Society, and Norman Eisen, chairman of Citizens for Responsibility and Ethics in Washington, speculated that Kavanaugh's "extreme views" on shielding Presidents from investigation were the key factor in Trump's decision to choose him as the nominee.[17] John Nichols, writing in *The Nation*, demanded that Kavanaugh pledge to recuse himself from "any deliberations involving Trump's alleged wrongdoing" in light of revelations that Trump's SCOTUS advisors had reviewed Kavanaugh's declarations on presidential investigations.[18]

In early August, additional controversy arose over how much of Kavanaugh's record would be released for consideration. Senator Mitch McConnell had warned Trump in early July that Kavanaugh's history in the Bush White House might lead to problems, as the Democrats on the Senate Judiciary Committee would surely demand to see all documentation of his exercises of duty in official positions.[19] By late July more than one million pages of documents had been released, including opinions and emails from Kavanaugh's career on the federal bench.[20] Despite this tsunami of paper, the pages did not include documents and records produced during Kavanaugh's five years of service in the George W. Bush White House, when he was first an associate, and then senior associate White House counsel.

Leading Democrats sent an independent letter to the National Archives requesting access to this material, which Senator Dianne Feinstein (D-CA) argued was "critical to understanding his knowledge of and involvement with torture, warrantless wiretapping, and the use of (presidential) signing statements, to name just a few key issues."[21] Ultimately, 415,000 additional pages of documents were made available

---

[17]Caroline Frederickson and Norman Eisen, "Will Kavanaugh Provide Cover for Trump?" *The New York Times*, 10 July 2018.

[18]John Nichols, "Brett Kavanaugh Once Argued That a Sitting President Should Be Above the Law," *The Nation*, 9 July 2018.

[19]Maggie Haberman and Jonathan Martin, "McConnell Tries to Nudge Trump Toward Two Supreme Court Options," *The New York Times*, 7 July 2018.

[20]Erin Kelly, "Senate Digs Through Record 1 Million Pages of Documents on Supreme Court Nominee Brett Kavanaugh," *USA Today*, 31 July 2018.

[21]Ibid.

through the Bush Presidential Library, but nearly 150,000 pages were identified as "committee confidential," allowing their review by Senators on the committee, but not their disclosure beyond the committee.[22] Just hours before the committee hearings began, an additional 42,000 pages were released for the confidential use of the committee.[23] While Democrats objected both to the lateness of the release and the continued lack of access to many parts of Kavanaugh's record, Republicans argued that the withheld documents were properly covered by executive privilege and moved ahead to conduct hearings.

While these issues fueled liberal objections to Kavanaugh, observers could be forgiven for seeing the process as heading for an inevitable confirmation. Kavanaugh had received a coveted "well qualified" rating from the American Bar Association, and the Republicans in the Senate were eager to complete his confirmation prior to the highly uncertain 2018 midterm elections.[24] Kavanaugh had by this point garnered public support from a variety of individuals and institutions from across the political spectrum. Among his supporters were prominent Democratic lawyer Lisa Blatt, former U.S. Solicitors General Ted Olson and Paul Clement, several former law clerks, and highly regarded liberal constitutional scholar Akhil Amar from Yale University.[25] Kavanaugh's boosters assembled a bipartisan group of supporters who submitted formal letters emphasizing his brilliance, even temperament, character, and willingness to hire and mentor women.[26]

When the confirmation hearings opened on September 4, the proceedings were somewhat tense. Democrats pressed Kavanaugh on abortion and on his involvement in the Bush White House, but Kavanaugh maintained his composure throughout. His confirmation

---

[22]Michael Kranish, "The Story Behind the Withheld Documents of the Kavanaugh Hearing," *The Washington Post*, 4 September 2018.

[23]Ibid.

[24]Debra Cassens Weiss, "ABA Committee Give Kavanaugh a Well-Qualified Rating," *ABA Journal*, 4 September 2018. The ABA would later withdraw this rating.

[25]Ibid.

[26]Senate Committee on the Judiciary, "Bipartisan Kavanaugh Advocates Send Flurry of Letters Supporting Nomination" Press Release. Washington, DC: Senate Committee on the Judiciary, 30 August 2018.

seemed assured, as no one predicted any significant likelihood of any of the Senate's fifty-one Republican Senators breaking ranks to vote against him.[27]

The Second Act: Christine Blasey Ford and Disturbing Allegations of Misconduct

Unknown to the general public, a different drama with a far less fixed script had been playing out behind the scenes. When Kavanaugh's nomination was announced, psychology professor Christine Blasey Ford called her congressional representative, Anna Eshoo (D-Palo Alto), and requested a meeting. On July 20, she met with Eshoo for an hour and a half, outlining a highly disturbing but in Eshoo's view completely credible claim that Kavanaugh had sexually assaulted her when both were teenagers.[28] Eshoo suggested that Ford detail the claim in writing and provide her account to Dianne Feinstein, the California Senator who was the most senior Democrat on the Senate Judiciary Committee. Ford accepted this advice and Eshoo's staff delivered the letter to Feinstein on July 30.[29]

The letter described the alleged assault in detail. Kavanaugh, Ford claimed, had pushed her into a bedroom and forced her down on a bed. He and another teenage boy had attempted to take her clothes off, with Kavanaugh holding his hand over her mouth. The other boy jumped on the bed, leading to a scuffle. Ford escaped, fleeing to a bathroom and locking herself in.[30]

Ford offered to speak with Feinstein but asked her to keep the letter confidential.[31] Shortly afterward, Ford retained attorney Debra Katz, a Washington, DC attorney with a reputation for defending

[27]Charlie Savage and Sheryl Gay Stolberg, "As Hearings End, Democrats Accuse Supreme Court Nominee of Dissembling," *The New York Times*, 7 September 2018.

[28]Casey Tolan, "Congresswoman Anna Eshoo First to Hear Blasey Ford's Story: 'I Told Her I Believed Her'," *The Mercury News*, 18 September 2018.

[29]Ibid.

[30]Christine Blasey Ford, "Read the Letter Christine Blasey Ford Sent Accusing Brett Kavanaugh of Sexual Misconduct," *CNN*, 17 September 2018.

[31]Ibid.

whistleblowers. Under Katz's advice, Ford took and passed a lie detector test.[32] Word began to get out among members of Congress about the letter, but Feinstein maintained confidentiality throughout August and into early September. The story broke in the national news media after the end of original hearings, with Feinstein confirming to CNN that she had information about alleged misconduct by Kavanaugh in high school, that the individual making the allegations had sought confidentiality, and that she had referred the matter to the FBI for investigation.[33] Democrats called for a pause in what they framed as a rush to confirmation, as Republicans criticized the Democrats' "11th hour attempt to delay."[34]

Ford told her story publicly a few days later, describing the assault and her subsequent efforts to deal with it in therapy.[35] She further revealed that she had contacted *The Washington Post* in July but had insisted upon maintaining confidentiality. She claimed further that she had decided not to come forward because she feared the disruption this would cause in her life, but the leaking of the story left her with little alternative. While Ford had no contemporary corroborators, her husband and three friends swore out affidavits in which they recounted her having told them about the assault prior to Kavanaugh's nomination for a Supreme Court seat.[36] Kavanaugh categorically denied the allegations and the White House declined to comment.[37] Kavanaugh's high school friend, Mark Judge, the second person in the room, also denied the allegations.[38]

On September 23, another woman, Deborah Ramirez, came forward describing an incident when she was in college. She recounted that Kavanaugh had "exposed himself at a drunken dormitory party, thrust

[32]Eli Watkins, "Timeline: How the Kavanaugh Accusations Have Unfolded," *CNN*, 17 September 2018.

[33]Ariane de Vogue and Phil Mattingly, "Democrats Send 'Information' Concerning Kavanaugh Nomination to FBI," *CNN*, 13 September 2018.

[34]Ibid.

[35]Emma Brown, "California Professor, Writer of Confidential Brett Kavanaugh Letter, Speaks Out About Her Allegations of Sexual Assault," *The Washington Post*, 16 September 2018.

[36]Glenn Kessler, "Brett Kavanaugh and Allegations of Sexual Misconduct: The Complete List," *The Washington Post*, 27 September 2018.

[37]Brown, "Professor Speaks Out."

[38]John McCormack, "Kavanaugh Classmate Named in Letter Strongly Denies Allegations of Misconduct," *Weekly Standard*, 14 September 2018.

his penis in her face, and caused her to touch it without her consent."[39] While no other witnesses corroborated the account, Kavanaugh's freshman year roommate confirmed that Kavanaugh had frequently consumed excessive alcohol and that he believed Ramirez.[40]

Finally, Julie Swetnick, represented by outspoken lawyer Michael Avenatti, submitted a sworn declaration that described a raucous house party scene among privileged high school students. She alleged that Mark Judge, Brett Kavanaugh, and others encouraged girls to become heavily inebriated and then engaged in serial sexual activity with them.[41] Her allegations became controversial after she appeared to change her story in an interview with NBC News and an ex-partner described her as both dramatic and erratic.[42]

Additional evidence was also proffered on both sides. For his part, Kavanaugh released his calendar from the summer in question, which had no mention of the party Ford had described. The 1983 yearbook for Georgetown Preparatory School, however, painted Kavanaugh in a different light. Photos and text made inside jokes about drinking and promiscuity and appeared to target an individual woman as a group sexual conquest.[43]

Ford's public allegations moved the consideration of Kavanaugh's nomination into a new phase. Ford's attorneys indicated to the Senate Judiciary Committee that she would be willing to testify, leading to days of "intense and closely watched legal wrangling."[44] Ultimately, the Judiciary Committee's Republican leadership agreed to a short additional hearing, offering both Ford and Kavanaugh the opportunity to tell their stories under oath, with the nation watching.[45] Prior to the

[39]Ronan Farrow and Jane Mayer, "Senate Democrats Investigate a New Allegation of Sexual Misconduct, from Brett Kavanaugh's College Years," New York, NY, 23 September 2018.

[40]Kessler, "Kavanaugh and Allegations of Misconduct."

[41]Ibid.

[42]Lia Eustachewich, "Third Kavanaugh Accuser Backs Away from Some of Her 'Gang Rape' Claims," New York Post, 2 October 2018.

[43]Kate Kelly and David Enrich, "Kavanaugh's Yearbook Page Is 'Horrible, Hurtful' to a Woman It Named," The New York Times, 24 September 2018.

[44]Sheryl Gay Stolberg and Nicholas Fandos, "Christine Blasey Ford Reaches Deal to Testify at Kavanaugh Hearing," The New York Times, 23 September 2018.

[45]Ibid.

hearing, Kavanaugh and his wife Ashley appeared together for a nation-ally televised Fox News interview in which he emotionally denied all of the allegations.[46] President Trump, reportedly unhappy with the cau-tious defense strategy pursued by Kavanaugh and his Senate supporters, unleashed a furious set of accusations against the Democrats, portraying Kavanaugh as the victim of a con game and witch hunt and Ford and the other accusers as liars.[47]

The hearing took place on Thursday September 27. Only Ford and Kavanaugh were invited to testify. Ford testified first, opening with a detailed, searing personal account of the assault and its monumental impact upon her life.[48] The Republicans, conscious of the highly pres-ent memory of the Anita Hill-Clarence Thomas hearings and their own demographic problem within the Judiciary Committee (all Republican members were white men), enlisted Arizona sex-crimes prosecutor Rachel Mitchell to handle the questioning from their side.[49] In accordance with the agreed upon rules, each Senator on the committee was allotted five minutes for questioning. The Democrats used their time primarily to speak to the nation about sexual abuse and secondarily to ask supportive questions to enhance Ford's narrative.[50] The Republicans ceded their time to Mitchell, who cautiously pressed Ford about the details of her narrative and suggested through her questions that Ford's costs were being covered by others.[51] Throughout, however, Ford maintained her narrative and repeated her certainty that Kavanaugh had attacked her.[52] Most observers agreed after Ford's testimony that she was sympathetic and credible.

[46]Kaitlan Collins, Jeff Zeleny, Kevin Liptak, and Dana Bash. "Increasingly Worried, Trump Takes Over Kavanaugh Defense," *CNN*, 26 September 2018.

[47]Ibid.

[48]Sheryl Gay Stolberg and Nicholas Fandos, "Brett Kavanaugh and Christine Blasey Ford Duel with Tears and Fury," *The New York Times*, 27 September 2018.

[49]Emily Tillett, Kathryn Watson, and Grace Segers, "Christine Blasey Ford Concludes Testimony, '100 Percent' Sure Kavanaugh Assaulted Her," *CBS News*, 27 September 2018.

[50]Emma Green, "The Kavanaugh Prosecutor is Asking a Baffling Line of Questions," *The Atlantic*, 27 September 2018.

[51]Ibid.

[52]Susan Page, "Analysis: On Kavanaugh vs. Ford, a Supreme Court Showdown Hinges on Whom You Believe," *USA Today*, 27 September 2018.

Kavanaugh's opening statement took an aggressive stance in response to the allegations. Rather than presenting an image of dignified denial, he described the confirmation process as "a national disgrace."[53] Angry, defiant, and tearful, he condemned the Democrats for destroying his family and name with "vicious and false additional allegations," and vowed that he would never withdraw or quit.[54] The format for Kavanaugh's questioning was the same as for Ford's, with the Senators receiving alternating five-minute slots. At first, the Republicans continued to rely on Mitchell to conduct questioning on their behalf, but Lindsey Graham (R-SC) reclaimed the microphone and engaged in his own show of temper.[55] He accused the Democrats of wanting power, staging a sham, and using Christine Blasey Ford to destroy Kavanaugh's life and retain the open Court seat for a future nominee.[56] When Democratic senators questioned Kavanaugh, he was resistant and dismissive, at one point retorting to Amy Klobuchar's (D-MN) question about whether he had ever blacked out after drinking, "Have you?"[57]

Reactions to Kavanaugh's testimony were sharply divided. Among the most positive responses to his aggressive pushback was Donald Trump's; Trump tweeted that "his testimony was powerful, honest, and riveting," and he repeated the claim that the second hearing was a "sham" foisted off on the country by the Democrats.[58] Uncertainty reigned; on September 28, the Judiciary Committee voted on partisan lines to advance the nomination to the Senate floor. However, Republican Senator Jeff Flake, a Kavanaugh supporter, was confronted in an elevator by two survivors of sexual violence, an event that may have proved critical in securing his support for further investigation.[59]

---

[53]Erin Schaff, "Updates from the Riveting Testimonies of Christine Blasey Ford and Brett Kavanaugh," *The New York Times*, 27 September 2018.

[54]Ibid.

[55]Green, "Prosecutor Asking Baffling Questions."

[56]Schaff, "Updates from Testimonies."

[57]Page, "Supreme Court Showdown."

[58]Schaff, "Updates from Testimonies."

[59]Sophie Tatum, "Brett Kavanaugh's Nomination: A Timeline," *CNN*, n.d.

The Committee agreed to ask Trump to implement a new FBI investigation into Ford's allegations, and Trump agreed to do so, stipulating that it would be "limited in scope and completed in less than one week."[60]

As the FBI investigation commenced, partisan tension continued to run high. The FBI did not speak publicly about its investigation, but news reports confirmed that agents had spoken with Deborah Ramirez (who claimed Kavanaugh had exposed himself to her at Yale), Mark Judge (whom Ford claimed had witnessed Kavanaugh's assault on her), and Leland Keyser, Patrick Smith, Chris Garrett, and Tim Gaudette (all of whom allegedly attended the party at which Ford claimed she was assaulted).[61] Trump publicly attacked Ford at a campaign rally in Mississippi, provoking criticism from Republican Senators Murkowski, Flake, and Collins.[62] The FBI's report was delivered to the Senate on October 4, and on October 5, the Senate conducted a procedural vote to advance the nomination, splitting on partisan lines. While interest groups and concerned citizens on both sides lobbied key Senators furiously, Kavanaugh was ultimately confirmed by a vote of 50–48 on October 7. One Democrat, West Virginia's Joe Manchin, voted to confirm, and Republican Senator Lisa Murkowski, who opposed Kavanaugh's confirmation, withdrew her vote to enable a Republican colleague to miss the vote to attend his daughter's wedding, maintaining a two-vote margin in Kavanaugh's favor.[63]

Kavanaugh's Confirmation and the Trump Court

The process that led to Kavanaugh's seating on the Supreme Court had some similarities to and differences from the struggle over Clarence Thomas's nomination in 1991. Like Thomas, Kavanaugh garnered opposition but looked to be relatively guaranteed confirmation during

---

[60]Ibid.

[61]Watkins, "FBI Interviews: Who Spoke in the Kavanaugh Investigation."

[62]Tatum, "Timeline."

[63]Ibid.

the initial phases. As with Thomas, the introduction of allegations of sexually related misconduct interrupted this process, leading to a dramatic face-off between the would-be Justice and his accuser. As in Thomas's situation, the public framing and hearings came down to a confrontation between Ford and Kavanaugh, despite the fact that other witnesses were ready to speak under oath about their recollections of Kavanaugh's behavior. In Thomas's case, the Senate Judiciary Committee knew about but never heard from Angela Wright, who also claimed to have been harassed by Thomas, and Kaye Savage, who had had an uncomfortable encounter with Thomas in his pornography-laden apartment.[64] Other witnesses would have corroborated Hill's allegations that Thomas had created a sexualized work environment, and Rose Jourdain stood by in case the committee wanted her testimony corroborating Wright's allegations.[65] They were never called. As Rose Jourdain later explained, "Thomas's supporters didn't want another woman, especially one with some of the same looks, age, and brains, telling a similar story as Anita Hill... Nobody wanted to deal with this."[66]

However, after Thomas's elevation to the Supreme Court in 1991, four women were elected to the U.S. Senate and a record number of women won election to the House.[67] While the Kavanaugh nomination and confirmation fight took place much closer to the midterms of 2018, those elections—conducted in the wake of more than a year of consciousness raising around the #MeToo campaign against sexual harassment and assault—saw a new record set for the number of women elected to the House.[68] Two Muslim women, Ilhan Omar and Rashida Tlaib, were the first elected to Congress, and Tennessee elected its first

---

[64]Jane Mayer and Jill Abrahamson, *Strange Justice: The Selling of Clarence Thomas* (New York: Houghton Mifflin, 1994).

[65]Ibid., pages 336–342.

[66]Ibid., page 343.

[67]Ibid., page 352.

[68]Samantha Cooney, "Here Are Some of the Women Who Made History in the Midterm Elections," *Time Magazine*, 19 November 2018.

woman Senator. Deb Haaland and Sharice Davids were the first Native American women elected to Congress, and Kristi Noem, a Republican, was the first woman elected as governor in South Dakota.[69]

The Hill-Thomas hearings provoked a national conversation about sexual harassment and contributed to the Senate's passage of a code of conduct barring harassment and creating congressional support for family leave and breast cancer research.[70] A few of Hill's most vigorous opponents paid political prices and some expressed regret for not having handled the hearings better and more fairly for Hill. Yet, ultimately, this new consciousness did not eradicate the problem, as the explosion of #MeToo testifies. In Kavanaugh's case, the national conversation was already well underway before Ford identified him as her sexual assailant. It is too soon yet to see if any policy changes will take place; a Republican-controlled Senate is unlikely to take action that reinforces the narrative that Ford was treated unfairly. Indeed, on November 15, the Department of Education proposed new regulations under Title IX that would afford more procedural rights to individuals charged with sexual misconduct or assault in an educational setting.[71] The person most likely to face a serious political consequence is probably Republican Senator Susan Collins, up for re-election in 2020, whose support for Kavanaugh enlisted widespread opposition and pledges to fund her opponent.

The Hill-Thomas hearings influenced what happened in 2018, and race played a different role in the dispute between Hill and Thomas than between Ford and Kavanaugh. Thomas, nominated to fill the seat vacated by historic black Justice Thurgood Marshall, had supporters within the black community despite his avowed conservatism, and relied on a narrative of his rise from humble, poverty-stricken, fatherless roots in an America just emerging from Jim Crow. In addition to

---

[69]Ibid.

[70]Mayer and Abrahamson, *Strange Justice*, page 353.

[71]Betsy De Vos, "Notice of Proposed Rulemaking," Department of Education, 15 November 2018.

claims that she was lying, Hill faced attempts to racialize her as incompetent, unstable, and sexually crazed.[72] Ford, while attacked by Trump, was handled more gently by other Republicans, who framed her as a pawn or tool of malevolent forces seeking to derail Kavanaugh's nomination illegitimately. Cognizant of the impression left by an all-male panel questioning Hill, the Senate Judiciary's Republicans opted to outsource their questions to the female prosecutor. Unlike Hill, whose opponents fairly uniformly painted her as a liar, Ford's opponents were more varied. In addition to claiming that she was an unwitting dupe, some claimed that she likely had indeed been assaulted but that Kavanaugh was not the assailant. Both she and Kavanaugh also hailed from highly privileged backgrounds, which shaped the narratives each was able to present.

One similarity stands out. Two years after his confirmation, Thomas allegedly declared to one of his clerks that he intended to remain on the Court until 2034 because "The liberals made my life miserable for 43 years, and I'm going to make their lives miserable for 43 years."[73] While it is too early to know how Justice Kavanaugh's jurisprudence will evolve on the bench, his angry demeanor and bitter denunciation of the Democrats for destroying his reputation are suggestive.

Kavanaugh's lengthy and deep connections to the Federalist Society and his strong association with Republican political figures already lent credence to speculation that he would be a reliable vote on the Court's conservative wing. Nothing that happened during the confirmation struggle dispelled this sense, and Kavanaugh's experience would seem, as with Thomas, to cement his alliances within the right-wing circles that he has inhabited throughout his professional life.

---

[72]The worst attack on Hill came in 1993 with the publication of David Brock's vituperative book *The Real Anita Hill*, which he later recanted. See Ellen Goodman, "Anita Hill 'Hit Man' Recants," *Boston Globe*, 1 July 2001.

[73]Neal Lewis, "2 Years After His Bruising Hearing, Justice Thomas Can Rarely Be Heard," *The New York Times*, 27 November 1993.

Beyond Kavanaugh, the hearings and subsequent events also seem likely to reinforce partisan rancor over nominations. Ultimately, partisan struggles over seating Justices raise the stakes on conversations about the Court's institutional role and its legitimacy, tying both increasingly to the political process. Trump's criticisms of "Obama judges" likely reinforced this perception, though Chief Justice Roberts has responded publicly in an attempt to reinforcing the Court's status as an authoritative but non-partisan referee.[74] While the outcome for the Court is uncertain, many Americans from divergent political perspectives will be watching Kavanaugh, Roberts, and the Court closely, with the cloud over Kavanaugh remaining undispersed for at least some of these observers.

---

[74]Jonathan Allen, "After Rare Rebuke, Trump Rips into Chief Justice John Roberts," *NBC News*, 22 November 2018.

Index

© The Editor(s) (if applicable) and The Author(s), under exclusive license to Springer Nature Switzerland AG 2019
D. Klein and M. Marietta (eds.), *SCOTUS 2018*, https://doi.org/10.1007/978-3-030-11255-4

Printed in the United States
By Bookmasters